GRAHAM REID

Born in Belfast, Graham Reid left school at the age of fifteen and took a variety of jobs before returning to full-time study at the age of twenty-six. After studying at the College of Business Studies and at Stranmillis College he graduated from Queen's University with a B.Ed. degree in 1977. He taught for three years in Gransha Boys' High School, Bangor. In 1980 he gave up teaching to concentrate on writing. Married in 1966, he has three children, two daughters and a son. All his stage plays have been given their first productions in Dublin. THE DEATH OF HUMPTY DUMPTY and THE CLOSED DOOR were first seen at the Peacock and Abbey Theatres. DOROTHY was given its first production at the Oscar Theatre, as part of the 1980 Dublin Theatre Festival. THE HIDDEN CURRICULUM, commissioned by the Abbey, was performed at the Peacock during April and May of this year. Two television plays, TOO LATE TO TALK TO BILLY and EASTER 2016, were screened as BBC Plays for Today in 1982. THE DEATH OF HUMPTY DUMPTY and THE CLOSED DOOR have both been published by CO-OPS BOOKS. Graham Reid has just been appointed Writer in Residence at Queen's University, Belfast.

0/1982

What they said about *Graham Reid*
"One of the foremost of this country's serious contemporary dramatists."
The Irish Times.

"He writes with such compelling power and passion that it seems to grip the audience and make it as taut as the play itself."
Sunday Independent.

D0995096

© Graham Reid, 1980, 1982.
ISBN 0 905441 53 2.

First published in 1982 by Co-Op Books (Publishing) Ltd.,
16, Lower Liffey Street, Dublin 1. Tel. 726329.

Co-Op Books acknowledges the assistance of The Arts Council (An Chomhairle Ealaoin) in the publication of this book.
Special thanks to Paddy Kane, Douglas Kennedy, Deirdre McQuillian, Finola O'Rourke, Miss K. O'Rourke.

Quote from *All Quiet on the Western Front* by Erich Maria Remarque by kind permission of Putnam & Co. Ltd.

Thanks to the estate of F. Manning, 1917, for poem included.

Design: Brendan Foreman.
Typesetting: Healyset.
Series Editors: Joseph Ambrose & Oliver O'Rourke.

"TOO LATE TO TALK TO BILLY"

For my wife
MARY
with love.

CAST

Norman	JAMES ELLIS
Billy	KENNETH BRANAGH
Lorna	BRÍD BRENNAN
Ann	TRACEY LYNCH
Maureen	AINÉ GORMAN
Janet	MAGGIE SHEVLIN
Stevie	WALTER McMONAGLE
Ian	COLUM CONVEY
Shirley	CHRISSIE COTTERILL
Mrs. Boyd	CATHERINE GIBSON
June Boyd	MARY JACKSON
John Fletcher	JOHN HEWITT

DIRECTED BY PAUL SEED

Designer:	DIANE MENAUL
Design Assistant:	MIKE SELINA
Costumes:	RODGER PARKER
Make-Up:	KATHY CARRUTH
Graphics:	IAN HEWITT
Props:	JOHN McCREADY
Scenic Supervisor:	DAVID McMURRAY
Engineering Manager:	WILLIE DAVIDSON
Lighting:	CLIVE THOMAS
	GEORGE CAMPBELL
Sound:	DIXIE DEANE
Senior Cameraman:	SAM WILSON
Cameramen:	JOHN OTTERSON
	JOHN CRAWFORD
	PETER COOPER
	IVAN LESLIE
Vision Mixer:	ANNE McCAW
Production Manager:	MARTIN PROCTOR
A.F.M.:	IAN HOPKINS
Production Assistant:	JENNY GORDON

1

Scene 1. THE CORNER OF A STREET
*The corner of a street of small two-up, two-down houses in the Donegall
Road area of Belfast. There is a shop on the corner. Ian is standing, dressed
in combat jacket and peaked denim cap. He has a stripe on his arm, new.
He holds two pick-axe handles. John Fletcher arrives, dressed likewise, but
with three stripes.*

IAN	Right John?
JOHN	It's sergeant on duty.
IAN	Oh aye, sorry . . . sergeant.
JOHN	Remember what that stripe means . . . you've an example to show.
	(Ian hands him one of the pick-axe handles)
	Rank means responsibilities, d'you read me?
IAN	Yes sergeant.
JOHN	Right . . . let's go.
	(They set off up the road. There should be a long view of the street that closes in on the exterior of the Martin's house, number sixty-three.)

Scene 2. THE MARTIN LIVING-ROOM.
*Lorna is ironing. There is a pile of finished clothes on the chair. She picks
up another garment, glances at herself in the large oval-shaped mirror
hanging above the mantleshelf, and then carries on.*

Scene 3. TINY SCULLERY
*Norman is shaving, his face lathered. His gear is laid out on the draining
board. He is using a small circular mirror, suspended from a nail.*

Scene 4. THE HOSPITAL SIDE WARD
Ann and Maureen, quite distressed, by their mother's bedside.

JANET	*(indistinct mumbling, then)* . . . for Norman. Are you there Sarah? *(to Maureen)* Sarah? *(Ann nudges Maureen)*
MAUREEN	Yes.
JANET	*(Mumbles indistinctly. Then)* Norman's coming.
MAUREEN	When are you coming home mummy?
JANET	*(Starts to cry softly.)* Norman's coming. Daddy doesn't allow me out.
	(Cries. Pause. She looks into Maureen's face. We see the nurse looking through the window. She moves towards her office door.)

2

I loved Stevie, but Norman couldn't understand that. I
loved Stevie.
*(Cries much harder now. Maureen starts to cry. A nurse
enters.)*
I loved Stevie . . . I loved Stevie, I loved him, etc. . . .
*(The nurse takes a tissue from her pocket and wipes
Maureen's tears. She ushers them out. As they go,
the nurse returns to Janet and talks quietly to her
holding her hand and wiping her eyes. We see Maureen
turn in the corridor to look back at her mother, Ann
puts her arm around her and leads her out.)*

Scene 5. THE MARTIN LIVING-ROOM.
*(Lorna is still ironing. Norman enters from the scullery, half his face
shaven.)*

NORMAN	Is that shirt near ready?
LORNA	It'll be ready when you are. You'd need to watch where you're going. The UDA seem to be at it all over today.
NORMAN	To hell with the UDA . . . So you worry about me now do you? *(Pause)* Just iron the bloody shirt.
LORNA	Are you going to the hospital tonight?
NORMAN	I've told you, I've a message to do.
LORNA	Dad . . .
NORMAN	Never mind all that. There's too many people in this house trying to tell me what to do. She doesn't know me half the time anyway.
LORNA	That's not the point . . .
NORMAN	Point my arse, you know what the point is . . . just smooth the shirt.
	(Lorna and Norman look at each other for a moment. He breaks away and goes back into the scullery. She finishes the shirt. He returns drying his face with the towel. She gives him the shirt and he starts to put it on.)
	Are my shoes polished?
LORNA	Yes, they're sitting beside your bed.
	(Pause)
NORMAN	Are you going up tonight?
LORNA	No. . . *(Pause)* . . . no . . .
NORMAN	No, and everything's understood and forgiven because you cry about it.
LORNA	It's not just that. I don't like leaving them at night, especially when there's trouble . . . I'll . . . I'll go up tomorrow afternoon. Billy'll maybe go up tonight. *(He takes a pound from his pocket and places it on the ironing board.)*

3

NORMAN	Aye, well, maybe he can get her a few grapes or something.
LORNA	She can't eat.
NORMAN	What! Oh aye. Well lemonade or something.
LORNA	Dad . . .
NORMAN	Look . . . I have to go out.
	(Pause)
	(He goes upstairs. She puts the pound into her pocket. She starts putting the ironing board down. She puts it into the scullery. Billy enters.)
LORNA	What's it like on the road?
BILLY	Normal. Roadblocks. Able-bodied men in hiding, the rest in uniform.
LORNA	Will you be all right to go up to the hospital tonight?
BILLY	Is he not going up?
LORNA	He's a message to do.
BILLY	A message! What about the rest of us. I'm supposed to be meeting June at half-seven.
LORNA	I'm sorry Billy, I'd go, but . . .
BILLY	No I'm not asking you to go. He should be going . . . him.
LORNA	Could you not wait until half-seven and take June with you?
BILLY	No . . . Jesus it's bad enough without having spectators.
	(Pause)
	I'll go . . . somebody has to be with her. I'll think of something about June. That lying oul frigger.
LORNA	Say nothing. He left a pound to get her grapes, or lemonade.
BILLY	Why didn't you tell him to stuff his conscience money.
LORNA	Billy, just drop it.
	(Norman comes downstairs, dressed in his suit. Combs his hair in the mirror above the mantleshelf.)
NORMAN	*(To Billy)* What's it like out?
BILLY	Don't know. I haven't had it out for days.
LORNA	It's quieter dad.
NORMAN	*(Pointedly to Billy)* Is the road still blocked?
BILLY	Why aren't you going up tonight?
NORMAN	I've asked you a question.
BILLY	And I've asked you one.
	(Norman and Billy glare at each other)
LORNA	Dad might be going up with me tomorrow.
NORMAN	Don't make excuses for me girl.
BILLY	There is no excuse for you da.
NORMAN	Am I accountable to you?
	(Pause)

4

| | Am I?
| | *(Billy turns away in disgust)*
| | Don't you question me boy. Don't you question where I go, or what I do.
| BILLY | *(Swinging round, angrily)* Your wife . . .
| LORNA | Billy! . . . (cont . . .)
| | *(Maureen enters. She senses the tension. Norman looks from Billy to her. He is going to speak, but thinks better of it. Pause.)*
| | Maureen . . . what kept you?
| NORMAN | I'm going.
| | *(He stands for a moment. Nobody speaks. He goes.)*
| LORNA | Where's Ann?
| MAUREEN | She's down at the corner gossiping
| LORNA | What kept you?
| MAUREEN | We were watching the soldiers taking a bus back.
| LORNA | That Ann one's no sense. How often have you two been told not to stand watching? When there's trouble you get straight home. That's how children get hurt.
| MAUREEN | I didn't get hurt.
| BILLY | Don't hang about again. You didn't get hurt this time but you mightn't be so lucky in future. Do you hear me?
| LORNA | There's no point getting at the child. It's that Ann one.

Scene 5A. STREET CORNER.

Ann and two school friends are standing watching as Ian is drilling half a dozen local teenage boys. John Fletcher looks on. Norman approaches. Ann sees him and runs home past him. Norman continues to approach John Fletcher and his troop. He walks straight on scattering them. We see John Fletcher's reaction of impotent rage.)

Scene 5B. THE MARTIN'S LIVING ROOM

Ann enters

| BILLY | *(Angrily)* The next time you're out with that child you get her straight home here. How many times have you been told not to stand gaping when there's trouble?
| ANN | Oh it was dead funny. The two soldiers took this bus and a wee drunk man came up and tried to give the soldier his fare. All the tyres were flat so then he tried to borra' a wee boy's bike pump. Then another big soldier came over, a cheeky big get, and knocked the wee man's money all over the road. I lifted ten pee.
| BILLY | Are you listening to what I'm saying to you?

5

ANN	It's all right, nobody saw me.
BILLY	I'm telling you not to hang about when there's trouble.
	(Ann slightly peeved that Billy is angry with her.)
ANN	All right, I heard you. There's no need to write a song about it. Here, if that wee drunk man had been my da, he'd have wrapped that soldier's rifle round his neck for him.
BILLY	The next time somebody might wrap something round your neck, and if they don't I bloody well will.
LORNA	Billy . . . Ann, I want you to go to the chippy. *(Pause)*
ANN	What do you want?
LORNA	Get two fish suppers and a chip, we'll divide them up.
BILLY	I don't want any.
LORNA	Why not, sure you've had no tea, you'll have to eat something.
BILLY	All right . . .
MAUREEN	Billy, my mummy kept calling me Sarah.
	(Billy looks helplessly from Maureen to Lorna.)
LORNA	She gets confused Maureen. She needs injections and they get her all confused . . . she needs them for the pain . . . *(Pause)*
MAUREEN	Who's Norman, Lorna? She kept on about Norman.
BILLY	You know bloody well Norman's my da.
MAUREEN	Oh, that Norman. I've never heard mummy call him that before.
BILLY	Was she asking why he wasn't up?
MAUREEN	I don't know what she was mumbling about.
	(Ann in defence of her father.)
ANN	He sent her up flowers.
BILLY	He must be practising for sending the wreath.
MAUREEN	What wreath?
LORNA	Billy!
	(To Maureen)
	Never you mind.
MAUREEN	She kept going on about Stevie . . .
LORNA	*(Firmly)* All right Maureen, that's enough for now. She didn't know what she was saying.
	(Billy and Lorna look at each other, both uncomfortable. Pause)
	Look . . . let's get our tea.
	(She gives the money to Ann.)
BILLY	Was Ian at the corner, Ann?
	(Ann pleased that Billy's anger at her has gone.)
ANN	Aye, he's all dressed up in his combat jacket and all, ordering all the wee lads around. John Fletcher's there

	too, the creep. If a real soldier comes up the road, you won't see them for dust.
BILLY	If Ian's there when you go down tell him I'd like to see him.
LORNA	Hurry up now, and watch that road.
	(Ann goes.)

Scene 6. MARTIN'S LIVING ROOM.
Just after they've eaten. Lorna is clearing up the plates.

LORNA	I'll put the kettle on for the dishes, Ann.
ANN	That fish was rotten, it was all batter.
BILLY	You can have him up, for too much a-salt and battery.
ANN	Billy, was that a joke, or are you just trying to talk?
MAUREEN	Lorna, can I go round to Sandra's house to see the film?
LORNA	What time's it over at?
MAUREEN	About ten I think.
LORNA	Ann can leave you round and then I'll collect you.
ANN	Am I allowed out?
BILLY	No.
ANN	Stuck in here all the time. I'm sick of it. All the rest are allowed out.
BILLY	You're not, and that's final.
ANN	If my ma was here . . .
LORNA	*(Sharply)* Ann . . . Mum's not here, and you're not going out.
	(Pause. Ian raps the door and enters. Still dressed in combat jacket, cap etc.)
BILLY	In the name of Jasus, what are you supposed to be?
IAN	Jealousy'll get you nowhere mate. Here, *(offers his arm)* look at that . . . eh?
BILLY	Somebody been chalking on you?
IAN	Chalk! What do you mean chalk? That's a stripe son, that's sewn on. No oul rubbish here.
ANN	Are you a general now Ian?
IAN	Close enough love, close enough.
BILLY	Is the alert over, or are the Martians still expected?
IAN	Eternal vigilantes, that's what Churchill said, and that's what we are.
BILLY	If the army catch you in that outfit they'll bounce you up to Castlereagh on your head.
LORNA	Would you like a cup of tea, Ian?
IAN	No thanks love, not when I'm on duty. What's wrong, you're not watching "Doctor Who" Maureen?

7

MAUREEN	The telly's broke' and the man from Gilmore's won't come to fix it 'cause my Da owes them money.
LORNA	Maureen, you don't tell your business to everyone.
MAUREEN	I didn't, I just told Ian.
IAN	Look at this stripe, Lorna. An officer and a gentleman now. My lips are sealed.
BILLY	They'd better be, or I'll take that stripe off and sew it across them.
LORNA	How's Shirley Ian?
IAN	Ah, she's all right. Still can't believe her luck at getting me.
LORNA	You two'll be getting married any day.
IAN	Married! Is your head cut? You'll not catch me getting married.
BILLY	If you start now you could have your own wee army before long.
IAN	Huh, I'd rather fight the next war on me own, than get an army that way. *(Pause)* What was it you wanted me for?
BILLY	I'm supposed to be meeting June at half-seven. But my Da can't make it . . . so now I'll have to go up to the hospital and see the old woman.
IAN	You want me to stand in for you do you? Let her have a real man for one night?
BILLY	Aye, I'm like that. Would you go and meet her and explain? Tell her I'm sorry. It's just my da had this important message to do otherwise . . . Tell her I'll call up to her house later. *(Pause)* Will you do that?
IAN	Aye, half-seven where?
BILLY	The corner of Tate's Avenue.
IAN	I'll just have to go and see the sergeant . . . it'll be all right, there'll be no problems, but I'll just have to let him know. I'll have to change too.
BILLY	You're joking, you mean you don't want her to see you looking all lovely in your uniform?
IAN	The name's Ian, not insane.
BILLY	Are you not seeing Shirley tonight?
IAN	Aye, I'm supposed to see her at half-seven. That's the time I'm off duty. Ah I'll tell her I'll see her later. I don't believe in giving women long explanations.
BILLY	I'll maybe see you if you're hanging about the corner when I get home.
IAN	Aye, all right.

8

Scene 7. THE BOYD'S FRONT PARLOUR
June is sitting at a table, applying lipstick. Her mother enters. Mrs Boyd is a woman, widowed, who manifests her love and concern for June through almost continuous nagging. She also employs a little moral blackmail by playing the ageing helpless widow.)

MRS BOYD	So you're going out after all.
JUNE	I can't just stand Billy up.
	(Pause)
MRS BOYD	You realise there's been trouble all over the town today.
JUNE	I'll be careful.
MRS BOYD	Careful's not enough in this place, you have to be lucky as well. You can't be lucky all the time. I thought we could just have had a quiet night here the two of us.
JUNE	I'm sorry mum, but we'll have lots of nights together.
MRS BOYD	Will we . . . just over a month and you'll be away altogether. I scimp and save and struggle to get you to University, but you can't go to the one just down the road. Not you, it has to be half-way across the world to suit you.
JUNE	Half-way across the world . . . York?
MRS BOYD	What's wrong with Queens, I'd like to know.
JUNE	There's nothing wrong with Queens, I just want to get away.
	(Mrs Boyd rises and crosses behind sofa.)
MRS BOYD	Now you're off out tonight and all this trouble. Anything could happen . . . you could be killed, then what would I do?
JUNE	Sure Mrs. Copper'll come in and sit with you.
MRS BOYD	And I'd have to sit and listen to the history of her aches and pains, no thank you. If you were never ill that woman would make you think you were dying.
	(Pause)
	Billy this and Billy that . . . you go and see Billy. I'll watch television, or read. It'll be practice for when you're not here at all.
JUNE	*(Pouting her lips)* What do you think of this lipstick?
MRS BOYD	It's all right . . . let's hope it's still on your lips when you get back.

9

Scene 8. THE STREET CORNER.
Ian is standing there. He has changed. Shirley approaches.

SHIRLEY	I thought you didn't come off until half-seven?
IAN	Aye, I had to get off a wee bit early. I've a message to do.
SHIRLEY	What sort of message?
IAN	Just a message, for a mate.
SHIRLEY	What about me? You're supposed to see me at half-seven.
IAN	I'll be a wee bit late . . . not much mind. I'll see you at half-eight.
SHIRLEY	Half-eight . . . that's a bloody hour.
IAN	Between half-eight and a quarter to nine.
SHIRLEY	Aye, keep it up. It'll soon be between half-eleven and a quarter to twelve. It's Saturday night you know. I'm not going to hang about waiting for you all night. What's this message anyway?
IAN	It's nothing love. Very hush, hush. Look I promise I'll be here by half-eight.
SHIRLEY	If you're not here by a quarter-past-eight . . . forget it.
IAN	Ah love . . .
SHIRLEY	Never mind the "Ah love" bit. I've heard it all before. If you're not here there'll be trouble.

Scene 9. MARTIN'S LIVING-ROOM.
Billy is ready to go out. Lorna hands him a sheet of paper.

LORNA	Here, take this. *(He opens it.)*
BILLY	What is it?
LORNA	Maureen made her a birthday card.
BILLY	Her birthday's not for over a week.
LORNA	Yes . . . I'd like her to have it . . . I'd like her to know . . . Just in case . . . *(She breaks down. Billy puts a hand on her shoulder. Ann comes in from the scullery.)*
ANN	What is it . . . what's wrong? *(Pause)*
LORNA	Have you all those dishes done?
ANN	Yes . . . why are you crying?
BILLY	I'm away . . . don't forget that wee girl.
LORNA	You be careful Billy. I wish you'd give June a miss for tonight.
BILLY	I'll be all right. I'll see you later. *(He goes. Lorna and Ann sit. They don't speak.)*

Scene 10. THE BANK AT THE CORNER OF TATE'S AVENUE.
June is standing. She checks her watch. Ian approaches, stops with her.
They speak for a moment. He has obviously given her the message.

JUNE	Well . . . thanks for coming up and letting me know.
IAN	No trouble.
	(Pause)
	Look, ah, why don't I walk you back up home?
JUNE	No, it's quite all right. It's not far.
IAN	Still, the oul troubles and all. I think Billy'd expect me to see you home safe.
JUNE	It's all right really . . . there's no need to.
IAN	No, I insist. Billy and me's best mates.
	(Putting an arm round her)
	You'll be all right with me.
	(June gently but firmly removing his arm.)
JUNE	I think it's better if we just walk together . . . in case you would trip, and pull me down with you.
	(They move off together.)

Scene 11. THE WAITING-ROOM BESIDE THE SIDE-WARD.
Billy is sitting gazing into space. Two nurses emerge from the side ward.
They are pushing a laundry skip. One nods to Billy and holds the door
for him. He gathers himself, as if going in is an effort of will. He passes in.
The nurses exchange a sympathetic glance and leave.

Scene 12. MARTIN'S LIVING-ROOM
Lorna and Ann are still sitting.

ANN	What will happen if Billy marries June and leaves? What will happen to us?
LORNA	We'll just have to manage without him.
ANN	Would you like him to marry her?
	(Long pause)
LORNA	No.
ANN	She wants him to go to England with her? Do you hate her?
LORNA	No, of course not.
ANN	Does he love her?
LORNA	I don't know. I don't think he knows.
ANN	Why do you not go out with boys?
	(Lorna is visibly upset, but doesn't reply. Pause)

11

Scene 13. THE BOYD'S FRONT PARLOUR.
June enters, followed by her mother.

MRS BOYD	Stood you up. That's a fine way to behave. Who does he think he is, standing up a daughter of mine?
JUNE	Mother, he did not stand me up. He sent his friend to tell me.
MRS BOYD	Sent his friend.
JUNE	He went to a great deal of trouble to let me know. *(Pause)* He's coming up here later.
MRS BOYD	Up here . . . tonight? What for?
JUNE	To see me . . . to talk
MRS BOYD	Really June . . . you know I don't like him up here.
JUNE	You're a snob mother.
MRS BOYD	I am not a snob. It's just . . . he's a boy I find it difficult to talk to. *(Pause)* Your father . . . well, we both wanted the best for you.
JUNE	Is telly good tonight?
MRS BOYD	Stands you up and then announces that he's going to stroll in here at all hours of the night. He wouldn't have done it in your father's time.
JUNE	Mother!
MRS BOYD	I'm just saying . . .
JUNE	Mother, I wasn't old enough for boyfriends in my father's time.
MRS BOYD	He wanted the best for you. He wouldn't have approved of Master Billy Martin.
JUNE	There's nothing wrong with Billy.
MRS BOYD	Nothing wrong! . . . He wouldn't have been allowed in over the door in your father's day. *(Pause)*
JUNE	Please . . . What did you do when I was out?
MRS BOYD	Well, I'd just turned the television off and settled down with a book, when Mrs Cooper called. Her sister's dropped in, and she'd run out of milk.
JUNE	She can't have stayed long.
MRS BOYD	Long enough to tell me about all her aches and pains. If that woman spent less time sitting on her own moping, if she'd get out more, she'd have fewer aches and pains.
JUNE	She's doing what you're threatening to do when I go.
MRS BOYD	Me! God forbid, you'd think that woman was in her seventies.
JUNE	Isn't she?
MRS BOYD	She is not, she's just a year or two older than I am. Her man ran after her too much, that was her trouble. God

JUNE	help him, there he is, gone this ten years and she's still here.
	I'd hate to see you like her.
MRS BOYD	Me . . . no fear . . . I'll be . . .
	(She looks at June, who is smiling.)
	It's only to have you here with me . . .
JUNE	I know . . . but sure if York doesn't work out after the first year . . .
MRS BOYD	You just remember you've got a home here. I want no daughter of mine starving herself, or sleeping in a dirty bed. *(Pause)* What about a cup of tea while you're waiting for Romeo?
JUNE	Lovely . . .

Scene 14. THE HOSPITAL

Billy emerges from the side ward. It should be obvious that the visit has been painful for him. He almost lies against the door. Punches the door-post. He looks back into the sideward. Turns, shakes his head. He moves slowly to a chair. He sits, and then with a long sigh he spreads himself out in the chair. He rests his neck on the back of the chair, gazing at the ceiling.

Scene 15. MARTIN LIVING ROOM.

Lorna enters with Maureen. She is removing Maureen's coat.

Maureen	Lorna, who was Stevie?
	(Lorna looking over Maureen's head at Ann whose expression is one of anger.)
LORNA	I don't know.
	(Pause)
ANN	I do.
LORNA	He was an insurance man who called every Friday night . . . that's all.
MAUREEN	Why does she keep on about him?
LORNA	I've told you . . . she just rambles. She doesn't know what she's saying.
ANN	*(Nastily)* He was her boyfriend.
LORNA	For goodness sake Ann.
ANN	It's true, isn't it?
LORNA	It was a long time ago. Maybe they were just messing around we don't know.
	(Quick fade)

13

Scene 16. FLASHBACK. THE LIVING-ROOM

The living-room some years earlier. Janet is sitting, dressed up.
Stevie enters, insurance books under his arm.

STEVIE	Come to the man who will "insure" your happiness.
JANET	You're late.
STEVIE	Unavoidably detained, one of those nights when nobody seems to have any change. *(In a mock Scottish accent)* Where's No . . . R . . . man?
JANET	Where he always is. I thought you were going to be too late. Young Billy's at a football match with his Uncle Andy.
STEVIE	I thought they went to bed early?
JANET	They do, but this is a birthday treat.
STEVIE	Is it young Billy's birthday?
JANET	No, it's Andy's. He always has a few drinks on his birthday. I always send him a card, which reminds him he's got a sister. Then he calls over and makes some vague wee generous gesture.
STEVIE	It isn't much, what does it cost for a youngster, ten, or fifteen pence?
JANET	Good grief, he's not that generous. It's taking him that's the gesture. He lifts him over. I even had to give him the money for a programme.
STEVIE	*(Grabbing her again)* Well let's not waste our time. *(Kisses her again)* We'll have to stop meeting like this darling. We'll have to change our "policy". Did you do what I told you?
JANET	I was at the doctor today.
STEVIE	Yes . . . well?
JANET	Oh, he wants me to go for tests. Probably nothing he says, but best be on the safe side.
STEVIE	There can't by anything wrong with you darling, because you grow more beautiful all the time. *(Pulls her closer)* I love you. *(Kisses her. Giggling is heard on the stairs. They break embarrassed. Feet are heard scampering up the stairs. Janet goes to the foot of the stairs.)*
JANET	Lorna! Ann! . . . If you two aren't asleep in two minutes I'll go up with the belt. *(Pause)* Bitches.
STEVIE	Will they tell?
JANET	No, no. I'll tell them it was only a joke or something. They're only youngsters.
STEVIE	*(Very worried)* But it might come out . . . they mightn't realise . . . good grief.

14

JANET	Oh come on . . . stop worrying.
STEVIE	I only sell insurance love, I don't buy any.
JANET	Listen, they wouldn't say anything that might cause trouble. Relax . . . *(Laughs)* . . . I'll "insure" we aren't discovered.
	(He smiles at her. They embrace again and are kissing when the door opens and Norman is there. Janet screams as Norman lunges at Stevie. Stevie pushes Janet aside and runs to scullery. Norman pursues him. Norman catches and throws him back into main room. Stevie falls over sofa to floor and Norman follows him.)

Scene 17. THE LIVING-ROOM
Back in the living-room now.

MAUREEN	What did daddy do?
ANN	He put Stevie bloody Wonder in hospital for six weeks, and he deserved it. It's all her fault. She used to tart herself up and go out to dances. That's what all the big rows were about.
MAUREEN	What was Stevie like? Was he nice?
LORNA	I don't remember. *(Pause)*
ANN	He wasn't when my Da was finished with him. It was awful. My da kept pushing his face against the wall. Then he punched my ma one right on the mouth.
LORNA	Dad walked out that night . . .; he didn't come back for two weeks.
ANN	That's why he doesn't visit her. I was with him and she said she loved Stevie, she said it to him. I thought he was going to cry . . . or kill her.
LORNA	It was a long time ago. People fall in love, it doesn't . . . *(Pause)* It started when Dad was in England. With his brother, Uncle Herbie, the builder. Dad worked for him.
ANN	She started him drinking heavy. She was always saying stupid things to men, and laughing when they said stupid things to her. Everytime you went out with her she'd stop to talk to some man. The whole street talked about her, laughed at us. Laughed at my da.
LORNA	Why should we care about the whole street?
ANN	Well I do. They tell you you look just like your ma, and then snigger about it. I'm glad my da gets drunk and knocks the shit out of them. It's all her fault, she was an oul whore.

15

LORNA	That's enough Ann. Just leave it. It's over and done with. *(Pause)* It's not as if she'll ever do it again.
ANN	Why did he come back at all after those two weeks?
LORNA	For us, he said.
MAUREEN	Then why does he hit us?
LORNA	It's the drink. *(Pause)* Men think all about the past when they're drunk.
ANN	I hate that oul bitch. You should have seen his face that day she said it. He looked at me . . . and I knew he hated me for hearing it. *(Pause)* Why couldn't we have a nice ma and da like Sally Johnston has?
MAUREEN	Uugh . . . They're stupid. They kiss at the door and walk about holding hands.
LORNA	That's what you do when you're in love.
MAUREEN	Uugh . . . but they're married and old.
ANN	They hardly even shout at her, and her da's never hit her.
MAUREEN	He wears an apron on Sundays and hoovers.
LORNA	Could you picture our dad in an apron? *(They laugh)*
ANN	With a wee feather duster . . .
MAUREEN	Out brushing the front . . .
LORNA	Could you picture them all round here if he did that?
ANN	If anybody said anything . . .
MAUREEN	Or laughed . . .
ANN	He'd ram the brush up their arses . . . *(They laugh)*

Scene 18. PUBLIC HOUSE.
Norman emerges with the woman. They are obviously having an argument. This should not be heard. She should walk away. He stands for a moment and then turns and walks away in the opposite direction.

Scene 19. HOSPITAL. WAITING ROOM.
Billy gathers himself. He goes and looks through the windows again. Holds a moment. Turns away. Leaves.)

Scene 20. DIFFERENT PUBLIC HOUSE.
Norman comes along – enters the public house.

16

Scene 21. BOYD'S FRONT-PARLOUR.
June enters with Billy. They kiss.

BILLY	Where is she?
JUNE	At the loo. She'll have heard the door and not be able to get down quickly enough. *(Pause)* How are you?
BILLY	I'm great, what about yourself?
JUNE	Great too. When you didn't turn up . . . when I saw him . . . How is your mother?
BILLY	Oh she's marvellous. Didn't you hear she played hockey today? It's true, cancer patients versus the rest. They are doing all right, until their sticks were removed. They thought they were malignant.
JUNE	I only asked.
	(She crosses to TV and switches it off, then returns to kneel beside Billy.)
	There's no need to be like that about it.
BILLY	I'm sick of it. Everytime I walk down the street they ask the same questions, and say the same stupid bloody things. Nobody cared much before. I've told you we're the joke family, remember? The drunken da, and the playgirl ma.
JUNE	Why do you resent sympathy?
	(Pause)
	That horrid friend of yours tried to pick me up.
BILLY	Ian? He couldn't pick up flu in an epidemic.
	(Pause. Mrs Boyd enters.)
MRS BOYD	Oh, you got here. I thought I heard the door.
BILLY	How are you Mrs Boyd?
MRS BOYD	I'm the same as usual . . . just the same. *(Pause)* I don't suppose you'll be staying long . . . in count of the trouble?
BILLY	It's pretty quiet now I think.
MRS BOYD	That's until the pubs get out. If they'd put a stop to the drinking. June's father always said it rotted mens' minds. The root of all evil he called it.
BILLY	I thought that was what money was supposed to be?
MRS BOYD	It's a mystery to me how the half of them can afford it. June's father never let a drop pass his lips.
BILLY	I don't drink either, Mrs Boyd.
MRS BOYD	Oh . . . have you stopped?
BILLY	I've never started.
MRS BOYD	Oh, well, you're a very wise young man. June's father always used to say that when the drunk man staggered in through the door, happiness left by the window. But of course you'd know all about that.

17

JUNE	Dad was a fund of knowledge.
MRS BOYD	He was a very clever, sober man. *(Long pause)* Do you go to church Billy?
BILLY	Ah . . . no . . . no I don't.
MRS BOYD	You should. It's a great comfort in times of trouble.
BILLY	Yes it must be.
MRS BOYD	How is your mother?
BILLY	She's very . . . *(Pause)* . . . she's very weak.
MRS BOYD	It's a terrible thing. Poor woman. *(Pause)* I had a cousin had the same thing.
BILLY	Yes . . . you told me about him before.
MRS BOYD	Him? Oh no, Myrtle . . . Our Myrtle had the same thing as your poor mother. Just thirty-six and with a young family.
JUNE	Mother . . . Billy will have to go soon, and we'd like to talk.
MRS BOYD	Yes . . . well I suppose . . . *(Pause)* She was just over four stone when the Lord decided to call her. *(Pause)* You should pray Billy.
BILLY	I am Mrs Boyd . . . hard.
MRS BOYD	I believe in prayer son . . . she laughs at me. You're not a Christian Billy?
JUNE	Mother . . . please. Billy doesn't have time for all this now.
MRS BOYD	Many a time prayer has worked when the doctors have given up.
BILLY	I must use your toilet.
JUNE	Would you like some tea?
BILLY	What?
JUNE	Pardon?
BILLY	*(Going)* The toilet . . . *(Pause)*
JUNE	Mother would you please go to bed without saying another word to Billy . . . please?
MRS BOYD	I was only trying to . . .
JUNE	I know, I know. He's just left his mother's bedside . . . he's very upset and it's the very last thing he wants to talk about.
MRS BOYD	Oh dear, was I tactless?
JUNE	He understands . . . but it's upsetting . . . it's just . . .
MRS BOYD	He says he prays.
JUNE	He's probably doing it right now.
MRS BOYD	What, in the bathroom? Surely he wouldn't pray from there? It's hardly decent.
JUNE	Come on mother. *(Rises)* I'm going to make Billy a cup of tea while you boil your milk.

18

(*They go. Pause. Billy returns. He crosses to the mantle-
piece and stares at the Boyd's wedding photo. He
replaces it as . . . June enters.*)
BILLY   Has she gone?
JUNE   Yes . . . I've a cup of tea on for you. I've just to take
up her cup of chocolate and then I'll be in with the
tea . . . (*They kiss. She goes.*)

Scene 22. THE HOSPITAL
*Norman staggers in and goes up to gaze into the sideward. He wipes
his eyes. After a moment a nurse enters and speaks to him. She gently
takes his arm and leads him out.*

Scene 23. MARTIN LIVING-ROOM.
*Maureen is curled up in a chair. She is dressed for bed, reading a book.
Lorna is polishing a pair of shoes. Another pair, already clean, sits
beside her. Two pairs, uncleaned, are on her other side. Ann emerges
from the scullery.*

ANN   Will I use butter or marge on the toast?
LORNA   Marge, and don't put too much tea in the pot. Hurry up,
I don't want you still at your supper when Dad comes in.

Scene 24. STREET CORNER.
*Ian and Shirley emerge from the entry and walk to the corner. They
are having a row.*

SHIRLEY You needn't think you can just turn up too late to take
me anywhere and just get that.
IAN   I've told you I got back as quick as I could.
SHIRLEY Going to see his bloody girlfriend for him. If I'd known
that's where you were going I wouldn't have waited
for you.
IAN   I just walked up with her. It was just the nice thing to
do.
SHIRLEY When do you ever do the nice thing for me?
IAN   Ah come on . . . didn't I bring you a present from
Bangor last week.
(*Shirley groping in her bag and bringing out a small
compact.*)

19

SHIRLEY	Present you call it . . . you got it cheap because the oul mirror was cracked. You probably looked in it.
	(She flings it against the wall.)
IAN	Ah you lousy wee bitch . . . that cost me money.
	(He gets down on his hands and knees to retrieve the pieces.)
SHIRLEY	You can count it paid for with the money you saved not taking me out the night.
	(She storms up the street.)
IAN	You've smashed the wee mirror.
	(He scrambles to his feet and starts after her.)
	Look at that . . . seven years bad luck . . .
	(A long shot of him catching up with her and her turning and kicking his leg.)

Scene 25. BOYD'S FRONT PARLOUR.
Billy and June are necking on the settee. He puts a hand under her blouse.
Puts it round to open her bra.

JUNE	Stop that.
BILLY	I've never been much good with bras.
JUNE	It's hardly worth the effort. I haven't got much there.
	(The heavy petting continues. He puts his hand up her skirt.)
BILLY	Come on June.
JUNE	No Billy . . . we shouldn't.
BILLY	Please love. Please. Come on . . .
JUNE	Oh Billy . . . I love you asking me. I love you . . .
BILLY	Come on June . . .
	(He pulls her onto the floor.)
JUNE	Oh Billy . . . Billy . . . oh . . . oh . . .
BILLY	It's all right love . . . that's it . . . that's it. It's all right June . . .

Scene 26. MARTIN LIVING-ROOM
They're at their supper. Lorna, Ann and Maureen. Ian is with them,
drinking tea.

| IAN | I told Billy I'd see him later. If I go into the house the oul doll'll start yapping if I go out again. *(Lifting up his trousers)* Look, Look where the bitch kicked me. |

20

ANN	Don't look so glum. This time tomorrow you'll kiss and make up.
IAN	Not this time. That's it . . .
LORNA	Come on Ian, sure you two are always at it.
IAN	Naw, this is serious. She took that wee compact thing I bought her smashed it against the wall. I mean imagine doing a thing like that.
ANN	That's seven years bad luck, breaking a mirror.
IAN	I told her that. She give me this boot on the leg and said she'd have the seven years bad luck going with me. *(Pause)*
LORNA	How did you get on with June?
IAN	Oh great, great. She was mad about me of course. But Billy's a mate, I didn't want to take her off him.
LORNA	You're so generous Ian.
IAN	Was he back down after the hosptial?
LORNA	No, he was just going on to see June.
IAN	I'm sorry about your oul woman, a mean I always liked her . . . I know her and my ma used to be always at it . . . but . . .

(He is becoming rather embarrassed and self-conscious. Pause. There is a loud roar from the street.)

(NORMAN'S VOICE: To hell with the hard men of Belfast. (cont.) Ian starts in alarm. Ian gulps down his tea and leaps to his feet, as Norman stumbles through door.)

NORMAN	Where is he?
IAN	You're all right now Norman. You're home now. Who're you looking for?
NORMAN	Don't you Norman me.

(He hits Ian on the chest, and sends him crashing against the wall.)

Respect . . . that's what I want, respect.
What are you doing in my house?

IAN	I'm ah . . . I'm waiting for Billy . . .
NORMAN	Where is he?
IAN	He's not here, not in yet.
NORMAN	Not here . . . not in yet. He's never here. Never bloody anywhere. Up seeing her, and out with girls, isn't he, eh? Doesn't matter about me. No time for me.

(Turns on a petrified Ian)

D'you think I'm a fool, son, eh? Oul drunk Norman, eh? I'll put you through that bloody wall . . . you and your da. It's Mr Martin you call me son . . . Mr Martin, d'you hear that?

(Ian nods)

21

LORNA	Come on Dad. Ian'll have to go home now. His mother'll be looking for him.
NORMAN	His mother! Mother nothing . . . his bloody oul ma. Y'know your ma can't talk about nobody. She serviced half the American fleet in her day. Maybe that's how you got your yella streak.
	(He holds his fist up to Ian's face.)
	You tell her if she talks about my wife again I'll smash her brains all over the nearest wall. You tell her my wife's a lady compared to her. You tell her my wife's near dead and she's still a better looking woman than her.
	(Pushing Ian towards the door. Shouting after him as he almost falls out through it.)
	You tell the oul bitch that. Near dead and she's still a better looking woman.
	(He slams the door closed. Pause.)
LORNA:	Right, come on you two, bed, quickly.
	(They rapidly finish their supper and leave.)
NORMAN:	That's right, the big wolf's here. You chase the kiddies off to bed. You're just like your ma.
LORNA	It's late dad.
	(He mimics her and swipes the abandoned dishes onto the floor.)
NORMAN:	It's late dad. Damn the late, I'm their father. Oh I know you might wish I wasn't, but I bloody well am. They're mine . . . my kids.
	(He staggers to the bottom of the stairs and calls our loudly.)
NORMAN	Ann . . . Maureen . . . come down here.
LORNA	Dad please.
NORMAN	Shut up. I want my children to kiss me night, night. Other men's children kiss them. I know what you and him are trying to do. Don't think I don't know.
	(The children enter sheepishly.)
NORMAN	Daddy wants a goodnight kiss.
	(The children look nervously at Lorna. She nods.)
	Never mind her. Never mind your big bloody sister, kiss me.
	(Maureen starts to cry.)
	What the hell are you crying for?
LORNA	Dad, please let them go to bed.
NORMAN:	You . . . it's you. You've turned them against their own father. This is my house. I've a right to be kissed by my own kids in my own house.
	(Maureen cries louder and he shouts louder than ever.)

22

NORMAN	Stop bloody crying.
LORNA	Leave them alone and let them go to bed.
NORMAN	Don't you tell me what to do. I'm sick of you telling me what to do.
	(As he goes for Lorna, Ann steps in between them. Before Norman realises what is happening Ann kisses him on the mouth.)
ANN	Goodnight daddy.
	(He stands stunned. Ann and Maureen go to bed. After a moment he lifts his hand and touches where she kissed.)
LORNA	Come and sit down dad.
	(Pause. She takes him by the arm and he lets himself be guided into an armchair. She sits on the arm of it and strokes his head. He takes her hand. He can't speak for a moment.)
NORMAN	*(Emotional)* It's too late Lorna. She's dying . . . I can't . . . can't . . . I can't talk to her. She doesn't know me. She doesn't understand what I'm saying. It is too late love, it is.
LORNA	Talk to Billy . . . talk to him . . . it's not too late for that.

Scene 27. THE BOYD'S FRONT PARLOUR.
Billy and June are sitting drinking tea. Silence.

JUNE	You're sorry you did it, aren't you?
BILLY	It's all right.
	(Long pause)
JUNE	That's it, isn't it?
BILLY	June I'm sorry.
JUNE	Thanks for buggar all. What does that make me? *(Pause)* I pity your mother if she expects sympathy from you.
BILLY	*(Angrily)* You leave my ma out of this.
JUNE	Yes, just let you do what you like and say nothing. Why don't you hit me Billy? Go on . . . hit me . . . that's the Martin answer to everything.
BILLY	Don't be stupid.
JUNE	I am stupid, haven't I proved that?
BILLY	I've said I'm sorry, what else can I say?
JUNE	Don't say anything Billy. Just show me you're human.

23

BILLY	I don't know if I'm human anymore. *(Long pause)* I can't go away with you June . . . not now . . . not yet.
JUNE	So that was the pay-off, your big finale?
BILLY	You could go to Queens. Give me time to sort things out.
JUNE	I could . . .
BILLY	Will you? *(Long pause)*
JUNE	You'd better go Billy. *(He rises)* Billy, for goodness sake be careful going home.

Scene 28. MARTIN'S LIVING-ROOM.
Norman is stretched out on the armchair, smoking, singing/moaning "Danny Boy". Lorna is sitting sewing. She checks the time.)

Scene 29. THE STREET CORNER.
(Ian is standing. John Fletcher staggers up)

IAN	Right John, what about you? *(John just nods and stands sullen. Ian looks uncomfortable.)*
JOHN	Where's your great mate Martin?
IAN	Billy, I don't know. I was just waiting to see if he'd come up the road.
JOHN	I'd a row with his oul fella.
IAN	He was in bad form the night.
JOHN	The oul bollocks is always in bad form. He hit me a dig on the gub.
IAN	He hit me too. *(John with contempt for Ian)*
JOHN	Hit you, what for?
IAN	He was drunk.
JOHN	I just ran on to a sucker punch, otherwise I'd have given him a good go.
IAN	He's tough.
JOHN	So am I . . . you saying I'm not?
IAN	No, no, you are John. You're one of the hardest men around here. I know that.
JOHN	I did your da one night. *(Pause)* I said I did your da.
IAN	I know, I remember.

JOHN	You want to get me for it, eh? You want to have a go?
IAN	No John, you give him a fair go.
	(John grabs him roughly and head-butts him. Ian's nose bleeds.)
JOHN	Your oul fella was easy, and so are you.
IAN	I didn't say anything John.
JOHN	You reckon I could take Billy?
IAN	I don't know, Billy can go some.
	(John drives him against the wall.)
JOHN	Could he take me?
IAN	Aaagh . . . I don't know John. *(Pause)* Please John, don't hit me.
JOHN	I'm going to kick your shite in.
	(Starts to drag him round the corner.) Come on round the entry.
IAN	Ah, please John, I never said anything, please.
JOHN	You're his mate.
	(Billy arrives on the scene.)
BILLY	What's going on?
JOHN	Oh, it's the Boy Wonder himself. Your great mate fancies his chances.
IAN	I don't . . . aaagh . . . I never said a word Billy. I was just standing waiting for you, I never said a thing.
BILLY	Leave him alone.
	(John slowly lets go of Ian.)
JOHN	Is that an order?
BILLY	It's good advice.
	(Pause. They glare at each other. John is not so sure anymore.)
JOHN	I'd a row with your da.
BILLY	He must have took pity on you if you're still able to stand.
JOHN	He hit me a lucky blow, before I was ready.
BILLY	My da could beat you with his cap.
	(Billy is anxious to avoid a fight, but he can't show any sign of weakness. This would seem like fear, and restore Fletcher's confidence.)
JOHN	You Martin's all think you're hard men, don't you?
BILLY	That's right, and we don't have to dress-up to prove it.
JOHN	Someday you'll push your luck too far.
BILLY	Anytime you want . . . like right now.
	(Pause)
JOHN	*(Laughing)* Look Billy oul son, I've had a bit too much.
	(He pulls a large bottle of wine from his pocket. Billy instinctively steps back a bit.)

25

	Trust me Billy. Listen . . . a wee drink, eh?
BILLY	I don't.
JOHN	Come on a wee slug won't hurt you. It was your oul
	fella I was mad at, but he got me a good one. Fair and
	square, he laid me out.
	(Offers the bottle)
BILLY	I've told you I don't.
JOHN	It's an insult to refuse a drink.
	*(He puts his other hand in his pocket. Billy notices
	this.)*
BILLY	All right . . . just one swig.
	*(Billy takes the bottle and crashes it down on John's
	skull. John slumps to the ground. Billy checks the
	pocket his hand went into and removes a flick-knife.)*
IAN	I think the rotten bastard's broken my nose.
BILLY	You don't gain anything trying to reason with the likes
	of him. You're better just lashing out and taking your
	chances. *(Pause)* I'm away up.
IAN	Are you going to leave him there?
BILLY	Why not, you don't think I'm going to take him home
	with me do you?
IAN	Should we not drag him into the entry out of the way?
BILLY	You do it if you like . . . he's your sergeant.
	*(Billy goes. Ian starts to drag John. He dumps him in
	the entry and comes back out.)*
IAN	*(Feeling his nose)* Bastard . . .
	*(He turns and goes back into the entry. The thuds can
	be heard as he kicks John.)*

Scene 30. MARTIN'S LIVING-ROOM
Norman sits up as Billy enters.

LORNA	Billy, where on earth have you been, it's after half-two.
BILLY	I got held up.
LORNA	There's no trouble is there?
BILLY	No, not a thing. All quiet in West Belfast.
	(Pause)
LORNA	How's mum?
	(He just shakes his head.)
NORMAN	I couldn't get away.
BILLY	I'll have to write to your agent and see if we can book
	you for the funeral.
LORNA	*(Quickly)* Would you like something to eat Billy?
BILLY	You just go to bed. I'll make myself a cup of tea.
LORNA	No, I'll do it.

26

NORMAN	*(Rising)* I'm going to bed.
LORNA	Would you like some tea Dad?
NORMAN	No, I don't want any of your tea. *(To Billy)* I was going to go up and see her tonight. I did . . . I had to see a man.
BILLY	Hurry up with the tea Lorna.
NORMAN	Are you listening to me?
BILLY	*(To Lorna)* Give me a round of bread and jam.
NORMAN	*(Grabbing Billy)* I'm talking to you. *(Billy pulling roughly away from him)*
BILLY	Why don't you go up to the hospital and talk to your wife?
NORMAN	Look, I'm trying to tell you. I'm trying to explain.
BILLY	Don't tell me, I don't want your explanations. Go up and tell her.
LORNA	Billy!
NORMAN	Tell him to listen to me.
BILLY	Why don't you tell me when you're sober . . . if I live that long.
NORMAN	I don't want any of your bloody lip boy.
BILLY	You might frighten those kids upstairs, but you don't frighten me.
NORMAN	I'm not trying to frighten anybody. *(To Lorna)* For Christ's sake tell him to listen to me. I'm trying to talk to him.
BILLY	You're about sixteen years too late.
LORNA	Billy, let him speak.
BILLY	I don't want to hear him. Go to bed old man. Go to bed and rest up for your wife's funeral.
NORMAN	I'll bloody kill you.
LORNA	Billy, the kids have had enough for one night. *(Pause)* Dad, look, leave it for tonight. Go up to bed and I'll bring you up some tea.
NORMAN	Shove your tea up your arse. You're always on his side. He's in the wrong, but you won't admit it. No, it's always my fault. Tell him, why don't you tell him he's in the wrong?
BILLY	Me in the wrong! What are you mouthing about you drunken idiot? You haven't been up to see my ma for over a week.
NORMAN	Your ma. You, and her, and your ma. I wish the whole bloody lot of you had cancer. I wish you were all bloody dying. I go out to work everyday. Your ma never knew what it was like to have a broken pay.
BILLY	No, but she knew what it was like to have a broken jaw, and a broken nose.

27

NORMAN	I'm warning you, I'm bloody warning you.
BILLY	Why didn't you let her run off with her insurance man?
LORNA	For goodness sake Billy
	(Billy shoves Lorna away)
	He was a better bloody man than you. At least he appreciated her. But you couldn't take that. She loved him. She despised you, but she loved him. *(Norman grabs him by the throat and knees him repeatedly, bellowing as he does so.)*

Scene 30A. MARTIN'S LIVING ROOM
Action of fight from end of dialogue through to end of Scene 32.

Scene 31. MARTIN'S LIVING-ROOM (FLASHBACK)
Norman kicking Stevie has a fistful of Stevie's hair. He keeps smashing Stevie's face into coalhouse wall. Janet attacks him, screaming. He drops Stevie to the ground turns and smashes his fist into Janet's face. She falls back into the scullery, flat out. He turns and starts to kick at Stevie.)

Scene 32. LIVING ROOM.
Stevie turns into Billy and we're back in the living-room.

NORMAN	I'll kill you, you wee bastard. I'll kill you. *(Lorna frantically tries to pull him off. When he stops, Billy is rolling on the floor moaning. Lorna slaps Norman's face. He grabs her hair and jerks her head back.)* Don't you ever lift your hand to me again, or I'll break your bloody neck. *(He pushes her aside, pulls Billy to his feet, drags him to the door. He throws him out into the street.)* If you ever come back into this house I'll kill you.

Scene 32A. EXT. MARTIN'S HOUSE (FILM)
Norman slams the door. Billy falling onto pavement and the front door slamming shut.

NORMAN	Shut up, up there. Do you hear me? Shut bloody up. *(Billy lies there.)*

28

Scene 33. SCULLERY FLOOR. (FLASHBACK)
Janet lying flat-out on the scullery floor, her mouth and nose bleeding.

Scene 34. HOSPITAL
Janet lying in the hospital bed, ashen, emaciated face and body. Staring blankly.

Scene 35. CHAIR.
Norman, cigarette in hand, slumped in his chair, gazing at the ceiling.

Scene 36. SCULLERY.
Lorna, in the scullery, crying silently, tears coursing down her cheeks. She is clearing up a few dishes.

Scene 37. CORNER (FILM)
Billy at the deserted corner. He stands for a moment, turns and limps off.

Scene 38. THE MARTIN LIVING-ROOM.
Norman is just finishing his breakfast, laid out on a small card table. (folding type). Lorna is taking a cup of tea.

NORMAN	What day's this? Tuesday isn't it?
LORNA	Yes.
NORMAN	Any word of that Billy fella?
LORNA	He called in yesterday.
NORMAN	Sneaked in when I was out?
LORNA	He shouldn't have to sneak in, it's his home.
NORMAN	When he's bringing in a wage to pay the rent it'll be his home.
LORNA	He gives all he can.
NORMAN	The dole won't keep a home.
LORNA	He does his bit dad, you know that. *(Pause)*
NORMAN	I writ to my brother Herbie a while ago. That letter yesterday . . . it was from him.
LORNA	I saw the Birmingham postmark.
NORMAN	He's a job for me . . . as soon as I want to go.
LORNA	And are you going to?
NORMAN	Why not? Damn all for me here. *(Pause)* I'll be away as soon as we see your ma off. *(Pause)* I'll not be back.

29

LORNA	We shouldn't give up hope. Mother might recover . . . God's good.
NORMAN	God's a bollocks!
LORNA	Dad! God forgive you!
NORMAN	*(Mimicing)* God's good . . . God forgive you . . . God bless you . . . God is love. Whoever he loves it isn't this family. He's never done nothing for us.
LORNA	You have to have faith.
NORMAN	Faith my arse. All your praying and church-going, hasn't done her much good. *(Pause)* When I was young I was dragged out to church three times every Sunday. My mother was the closest thing to a saint you'll ever see. My da was a drunken waster. Before she got out to church on a Sunday morning she'd have to wash the spew from him and put him to bed. He died in his sleep on a Tuesday night, with a smile on his face. *(Pause)* Do you know what happened to her?
LORNA	You've told me.
NORMAN	Well I'll tell you again . . . she lay for months in agony. I heard her praying . . . for relief. I heard her praying to die. For the last week of her life she screamed at him to help her. There was no smile on her face when she died. Her face was twisted up in pain. *(Pause)* Don't you tell me God is good, girl.
LORNA	Maybe the reason't not for us to know.
NORMAN	Aye, he's a great one for keeping secrets. Do you know what they told me? They said God was trying to spare me. He didn't want me to mourn my mother, so he made it that awful I'd be glad to see her going. Did you ever hear such a load of oul nonsense in your life?
LORNA	I wish you wouldn't talk like that. You never know what might happen to you when you step out of that door. *(Pause)* Would you like some more tea?
NORMAN	*(Draining his cup)* Aye . . . a half cup.
	(She takes his cup and goes into the scullery to refill it. He starts tying his boots. She returns.)
LORNA	Dad?
NORMAN	I said half a cup, that's three quarters. *(Sips)* What?
LORNA	Can Billy come back?
NORMAN	I've told you I'm going. After that you and him's in charge. *(Pause)*
LORNA	He'll have to come up soon for clothes, but I'd like him back.
NORMAN	Where's he staying anyway?

30

LORNA	He's with Uncle Andy.
NORMAN	Huh, I wouldn't wish that dirty oul frigger even on him. Does he still fart and blame the cat? *(Pause)* Tell him he can come back . . . that I'll be going away soon.
LORNA	Thanks dad.
	(She goes into the scullery. He rises, drains his cup, combs his hair, and puts on his jacket and overcoat. She returns with his lunchbox.)
NORMAN	What's in them?
LORNA	Chicken paste.
NORMAN	Is there a bun for my tea break?
LORNA	There's two custards.
NORMAN	It's time you got yourself a boyfriend you know . . . you can't waste your own life on the others. *(Pause)* Don't tell them two young ones I'm goin', not until nearer the time.
	(He stands with the door open, ready to go. She kisses him on the cheek.)
LORNA	Take care of yourself dad.
NORMAN	I'm only going to the bloody shipyard, not the Western Front.
	(He goes.)

Scene 39. ENTRANCE TO BOTANIC GARDENS (FILM)
(Billy and Lorna emerge from the front gates of Botanic Gardens. They cross the road and stroll up College Gardens. Fade up on dialogue from)

LORNA	Ian's gone. Nobody knows where he is, just disappeared. John Fletcher has a fractured skull. The police are at his bedside.
BILLY	Do they know what happened to him?
LORNA	They know he was hit over the head, probably with a bottle, but he was kicked as well. Apparently he could be barely recognised. His face was kicked to a pulp.
BILLY	Will he live?
LORNA	Nobody knows. It happened on Saturday. This is Tuesday and he's still unconscious. It could have been you, walking over to Uncle Andy's at that time of night.
BILLY	I was all right, I'm not involved in anything.
LORNA	What does that matter? What did Uncle Andy say to you?
BILLY	Oh the usual . . . about his poor sister and the bad man she married.
LORNA	I could laught at him and his "poor sister" bit, he never had much time for her . . .

31

Scene 40. LISBURN ROAD/CITY HOSPITAL. (FILM)
(Billy and Lorna walk across the Lisburn Road, and into the grounds of the city hospital. Fade up on dialogue, from)

BILLY	And my da said I could come back?
LORNA	Yes. *(Pause)* It was terrible after he'd gone to bed on Saturday. I heard him arguing with himself . . . and then he started crying.
BILLY	He must have got all the draws and forgot to post the coupon.
LORNA	He's like a bear with a thorn in it's paw, and he doesn't know how to get it out.
BILLY	We should be drilling through the top of his head.
LORNA	He really did want to talk to you the other night. I wish you'd listened.
BILLY	We can't talk Lorna. Maybe we should phone each other or something.
LORNA	You can maybe add a few lines to the bottom of my letters when he goes away?
BILLY	Aye . . . maybe. *(Pause)* When he hands over to me.

Scene 41. SIDE-WARD.
Billy and Lorna approach the side-ward.

LORNA	Billy . . . *(They stop)* . . . do you believe in God? *(Billy gazing through side-ward window. He looks back at Lorna.)*
BILLY	No.
LORNA	What do you think of people who do?
BILLY	They're lucky. *(They pass into the side-ward.)*

Scene 42. THE MARTIN'S LIVING-ROOM.
The Martin living room. Billy and Lorna are taking a cup of tea. Ann and Maureen enter.

BILLY	Hello girls.
ANN	Billy, have you moved back in?
BILLY	Yep.
ANN	Great, how was life with Uncle Andy?

32

BILLY	It's a great way to slim. By the time he's finished spitting his lungs up into the fire, and taking his teeth out and setting them beside his plate, the appetite just leaves you.
LORNA	Oh Billy . . .
MAUREEN	I'm away out again Lorna.
LORNA	You watch where you're going, and be in for your tea. *(She goes)*
BILLY	How's school Ann?
ANN	Uuugh. The Concorde says I've to get my da to sign all my homeworks.
BILLY	Who's the Concorde?
ANN	Mr. Williamson. You should see his hooter. When he's turned sideways he looks just like the Concorde. I told him my da wouldn't do it, but he says it has to be him or my ma, nobody else.
LORNA	I'll sign Dad's name, sure he'll never know the difference.
ANN	With a snout like his he'd smell a rat at twenty thousand feet.
BILLY	You should have asked him round to meet my da. Being a teacher he probably thinks most dads are human.
ANN	I'd love to. My da'd probably get him by the big snout and swing him round his head.
LORNA	Why does he want your homework signed all of a sudden?
ANN	It's just about ten ot us. He said our attitude was . . . what was it now? . . . submersive, or something daft like that.
LORNA	Do you not think we've enough to worry about without any trouble from the school?
ANN	It's not my fault.
LORNA	You keep out of trouble. If he sends a note home to Dad, you're dead. Is he new?
ANN	Aye . . . he's a drip and he thinks he's lovely. Keeps chatting up Miss Baker. It's a laugh. Sandra Mercer said to Miss Baker the other day, "Excuse me Miss, Baker, have you ever had a ride by Concorde?" We were killing ourselves, but she didn't catch on. "As a matter of fact Mercer, I was thinking of trying it next summer."
LORNA	I'm warning you Ann, don't get into any trouble up there. *(Pause)*
LORNA	Are you going up again Billy?
BILLY	Aye, I'd better.
ANN	Are you not seeing June?
BILLY	No . . . not tonight.
ANN	Why do you never bring her down now Billy?

BILLY	She's going away soon.
	(Long pause)
ANN	Are you going with her?
LORNA	Never mind all the questions Ann, you'd . . .
BILLY	No . . . I'm staying here.
	(He looks at Lorna. They smile.)

Scene 43. STREET. (FILM)
Billy coming down the street. He meets Ann on her way home from school. They speak. She appears to break down and go racing up the street. He continues down the street.

Scene 44. THE MARTIN'S LIVING-ROOM.
The Martin Living-room. Lorna is at the sink. Ann tumbles in upset. She drops her schoolbag. They gaze at each other for a moment. Pause.

ANN	Is she dead?
LORNA	Not quite . . . Billy's away up.
ANN	I saw him . . . he wouldn't say . . . where's my da?
LORNA	He's not home yet. They've sent for him.
ANN	Is he still going away?
LORNA	Yes.
ANN	I don't want him to go. Who'll look after him over there?
LORNA	Sush love . . . let's get this bit over first.
ANN	Are we going up?
LORNA	Billy says no. *(Pause)* I'd rather not anyway.
	(Pause. Ann collapses into Lorna's arms.)

Scene 45. SIDE-WARD.
Billy outside the side-ward. A nurse opens the door of the side-ward and beckons him in.

Scene 46. THE MARTIN'S LIVING-ROOM.
The Martin's Living-room. June is there.

JUNE	Do you think it would be all right?
LORNA	It'll be all right . . . he'll be glad of someone. *(Pause)*
	I can't . . .
	(Pause)
JUNE	Thank you . . .
	(She goes)

Scene 47. SIDE-WARD.
Norman gazes through the sideward window. After a moment he enters.
Billy looks up at him. Norman looks at the bed.

Scene 47A. MARTIN'S LIVING-ROOM.
Norman sees Janet laughing

Scene 47B. SCULLERY, MARTIN HOUSE.
Janet lying on the scullery floor bleeding.

Scene 47C. SIDE-WARD.
Janet as she is — dead.

BILLY	You've mistimed it again. You're too late to talk to her, and too early for the funeral. I suppose you'd difficulty finding your way?
NORMAN	I'd like to talk to her.
BILLY	She's dead . . . you're too late.
NORMAN	Please son . . . give me a minute with her . . . *(Billy turns and walks away. Then turns back as Norman breaks down. Billy watches then continues exit to join June in extreme little side-ward.)*

Scene 48. WAITING ROOM.
Billy comes back into the little waiting room. His left hand is tightly closed.
June is there. He sits.

BILLY	I've never saw a corpse before. She looked sort of surprised. Strange . . . sort of look on her face. She must have been dead nearly half-an-hour before I realised. *(He opens his left hand to reveal her rings.)* She wanted Lorna to have these.
JUNE	I called at the house. Lorna told me. I hope you don't mind . . .
BILLY	He turned up late, and stinking of drink. It's funny, the last thing I heard her saying was, "His bloody dinner's going to be cold again."
JUNE	That was nice, she was thinking about him at the end.
BILLY	He's in there now . . . all this time, and he waits until she's dead before he tries to talk to her!

35

JUNE	If I was married to someone all those years, I wouldn't want to come up here and watch them dying for an hour every night.
BILLY	What was your da like?
JUNE	An old man, I never knew him as anything else. I should have been his grandaughter . . . so we never really got anything going.
BILLY	They're the lonliest places in the world these hospitals. Listen. *(Silence)*
JUNE	I've made up my mind Billy. I came to tell you. *(Pause)*
JUNE	I'm going to York.
BILLY	They need me . . .
JUNE	I could stay for you and never be certain. Then I'd have four years of my mother, as well as the troubles. Maybe all for nothing.
BILLY	My da's going back to England. His brother's a builder. He's going back to work with him.
JUNE	My mother told me I'd not find many young Christians men like you in England. *(Long pause)* She'll be fine.
BILLY	You'll come back for holidays?
JUNE	Yes . . . and we can write.

Scene 49. ENTRANCE TO THE HOSPITAL. (FILM)
Billy and June approach the Lisburn Road entrance to the hospital.

| BILLY | I'll walk you home. |
| JUNE | No. *(She kisses him quickly.)* I'll send my address. *(She goes. He watches her for a moment, then turns and walks down the road.)* |

Scene 51. THE MARTIN LIVING-ROOM.
Billy is sitting. Lorna, Ann and Maureen are standing. Norman's two suitcases are sitting on the floor. Lorna is holding a package that contains sandwiches. Norman comes down the stairs. He wears a suit and is carrying an overcoat, which he now puts on. Checks his hair in the mirror.

| NORMAN | That's it . . . all set. *(Pause)* |
| LORNA | I've made you a few sandwiches. |

36

ANN	Will you write to me da?
MAUREEN	And me . . .
NORMAN	In the name of Jasus . . . I'm going over there to work, not to write letters. *(Pause)* I'll write to Lorna.
LORNA	Have you a clean hankie?
NORMAN	Aye. *(Ill at ease. Pause)* You two young ones now, be good. I don't want any bad reports. Watch your school and all. Right. *(He goes awkwardly and kisses Ann and Maureen.)*
ANN	You be careful da.
NORMAN	I'll be fine. *(Billy rises and picks up one of the cases. Lorna hands Norman the sandwiches, and they kiss.)*
BILLY	*(Gesturing to the case.)* I know you're going to work on a building site, but you don't have to bring your own bricks.
NORMAN	Here . . . you take this one, it's not too bad.
BILLY	Naw, it's all right. *(Moving to the door.)*
NORMAN	Wait a minute. *(He opens the case he carries and squeezes the sandwiches in.)*
LORNA	They'll not be worth eating by the time you've done.
NORMAN	What's in them?
LORNA	Some chicken paste, and some cheese. There's a few buns too.
MAUREEN	Just say the boat sinks?
NORMAN	I'll thumb a lift in a submarine. Right . . . *(To Billy)* . . . are you ready? *(Billy nods.)*
LORNA	Scribble a wee note as soon as you're there and let us know you're safe, won't you?
NORMAN	Aye . . . aye . . . *(They go)*

Scene 52. STREET. (FILM)
Norman and Billy walking down the street, Lorna, Ann and Maureen, stand at the front watching. Half way down Norman turns for a last wave, but the two younger girls are already playing a game, Lorna waves. They turn again.)

Scene 52A. MARTIN'S LIVING-ROOM.
Lorna re-entering house.

Scene 52B. CITY CENTRE. (FILM)
Norman and Billy walking towards P & O terminal.

Scene 52C. MARTIN'S LIVING-ROOM.
Lorna still clearing up. Maureen and Ann come in.

Scene 52D. FERRY TERMINAL. FILM
The P & O ferry terminal at Belfast harbour. Inside.

BILLY	You'd better go that was the last call. *(Puts out his hand.)*
NORMAN	*(Taking Billy's hand.)* Yesterday under that coffin's the first time we've had our arms around each other since you were two or three.
BILLY	Stay off the drink da.
NORMAN	We made a right pig's arse of it, me and your mother. *(Pause)* Take care of them for me son. *(Pause).* This is the best way.
BILLY	The only way. *(Norman moves as if to embrace him. Billy takes a half step back.)*
BILLY	Good luck da. *(They part)*

Scene 52E. P & O FERRY TERMINAL (FILM)
Billy exits cafeteria. Walks down stairs and through exit doors.

Scene 53. P & O TERMINAL – GANGWAY (FILM)
Norman walks along gangway. Turns for a final look towards P & O building then continues towards ferry.

Scene 53A. MARTIN'S LIVING-ROOM.
Ann doing dishes. Lorna putting Maureen into her pyjamas. T.V. on.

Scene 53B. P & O TERMINAL (FILM)
Norman on boat rail.

Scene 53C. QUEEN ELIZABETH BRIDGE (FILM)
Billy on the Queen Elizabeth Bridge gazing at the boat. Long shot of boat in harbour.

Scene 53D. MARTIN'S LIVING-ROOM.
Lorna, with Ann, watching T.V. Maureen asleep.

Scene 54. QUEEN ELIZABETH BRIDGE (FILM)
Boat pulling out. Billy walking away.

Scene 54A. MARTIN'S LIVING ROOM.
Lorna carrying Maureen asleep upstairs. Ann watching TV/making toast.

Scene 54B. EXT. CITY HALL (FILM)
Billy passing City Hall.

Scene 54C. MARTIN LIVING ROOM (STUDIO)
Ann kissing Lorna goodnight. Lorna doing sewing.

Scene 54D. STREET CORNER. (FILM)
Billy passing the deserted corner.

Scene 55. MARTIN'S LIVING-ROOM.
*Billy enters. He looks at Lorna for a moment. She is holding her parents'
framed wedding photograph, about to put it away. The others have
gone to bed. He takes the photograph from her, looks at it and sets it
on the mantleshelf. For the first time in many years.*

LORNA	Are you going to leave it there?
BILLY	That's where it belongs. It's the only way we can all be together in this house.
LORNA	Maureen'll wonder who they are. *(Pause)* He left me some money, and said he'd send some. *(Pause)*
BILLY	That day in the hospital, when she died . . . he took her hand. *(Pause)* I thought he was singing to her . . . but he was crying . . . like a dog whining . . .
LORNA	*(With a slight smile)* He used to sing to her . . . do you remember? *(Go out on Norman singing/moaning "Danny Boy" as the shot closes in on the photograph.)*

Scene 56. MARTIN LIVING ROOM.

BILLY	She always used to sing. When she was cooking anything she'd always be singing *(Pause)*. Then she stopped. *(Pause)*
LORNA	*(Moving around)* I'd better check their stuff for the morning. Maureen tore her blouse. I hope there's white thread.
BILLY	You do that and I'll make our supper. *(Pause) (Lightly)* We'll have toast, for a change.
LORNA	Right . . . you can use butter on it. I kept it for dad's pieces.

BILLY	I'll take you and the kids up to see the grave next Sunday.
LORNA	Yes . . . I want it kept nice. We could plant flowers on it . . . it'd be like a wee garden. *(F/X fade up into bar on ferry.)*
A VOICE	There y'are Norman.
NORMAN	Thanks, Cheers.
VOICE	I saw it in the paper right enough. Was she bad long?
NORMAN	Aye a long time. We were expecting it you know.
VOICE	Aye . . . still its always a bit of a shock when it comes. It's rough on the kids — losing a mother, like.
NORMAN	It is . . . I've great wee youngsters there mind.
VOICE	Able to look after themselves and all?
NORMAN	What . . . that eldest girl of mine's like a mother to the rest of them. She's looked after the lot of us this past couple of years.
VOICE	It's great to have one like that right enough.
NORMAN	And my young lad . . . Billy . . . great wee fella. They'll keep things going alright. No problems that way. *(Pause)* Great youngsters, I'm luck that way.

DOROTHY

For Nora Reid
June 23, 1919
June 3, 1981
The Last One She Saw

CAST

DOROTHY WILLIAMS: About fifty. Very attractive.

CHARLES WILLIAMS: Her husband, Fifties. Small builder.

DOUGLAS WILLIAMS: Her son. Early twenties. Student.

DORIS: Her sister. Forty-sevenish. Plain.

STEPHEN MONTGOMERY: Early twenties. Ex-friend of Douglas. Student.

MIKE: Late twenties.

ANDY: Late twenties.

CASTING

DOROTHY   =   JOAN O'HARA

CHARLES   =   GODFREY QUIGLEY

DOUGLAS   =   DENIS STAUNTON

DORIS   =   ENA MAY

STEPHEN   =   GERARD McSORLEY

MIKE   =   MAURIE TAYLOR

ANDY   =   DEREK LORD

Directed by =   KEVIN McHUGH

Designed by =   ROBERT LANE

Costumes by =   JULIET WATKINSON

41

SCENE 1

THE LIVING-ROOM OF A LUXURY
BUNGALOW IN A MIDDLE-CLASS SUBURB OF BELFAST.
*The bungalow is situated on a hill overlooking the city and the Lough.
The room is tastefully furnished. There should be a drinks cabinet and
a telephone. On the table beside the telephone is a large framed
photograph of a grinning Charles. There should be two exits from the
room. One leads to the front door, bathroom and toilet, and Douglas'
bedroom. The other gives access to the master toilet, working kitchen,
and through the working kitchen to the back garden. The telephone is
ringing as lights come up. Dorothy appears slowly from the bedroom. She
seems reluctant to lift the receiver, and in the end snatches it up.*

DOROTHY   Hello . . . Oh God. Look, who is that? . . . I don't know
                 who you are. Pardon? Please, just leave me alone . . . If
                 you don't stop pestering me I'm going to call the
                 police . . . No . . . Look how do you know that? . . .
                 Who are you?

*The caller hangs up. She slams down the receiver and lights a cigarette. She
presses on the cassette, Don Williams singing "Gipsy Woman", and appears
to listen to it intently. The doorbell rings, startling her. She turns off the
cassette and stubs out her cigarette, touches up her hair and adjusts
herself before going to the door. She returns with Doris. Doris is a few
years younger than Dorothy, but if anything looks slightly older. She
wears glasses, and by comparison, drab, somewhat old fashioned clothes.
A "sensible tweeds" type.*

DOROTHY   I thought you were Charles, he's always forgetting his
                 key.

DORIS   Surely he'd never be home as early as this?

DOROTHY   We're going to a dinner dance at the university tonight.
                 They should be here anytime.

DORIS   Is Douglas going too?

DOROTHY   Yes. It's one of my treats, to compensate me for all the
                 weekends they're away.

DORIS   That'll be nice. You don't seem to get out as often as you
                 used to.

DOROTHY   Not during the football season. Then in the brighter
                 nights there's all the overtime on the site.

(The telephone rings again. Dorothy visibly jumps. She rushes over and snatches it up.)
Hello, hello . . . no . . . I'm sorry, you've got a wrong number.
(She crashes the phone down.)

DORIS	Here, are you all right girl? Who was that?
DOROTHY	Wrong number, somebody . . . would you like a drink?
DORIS	Are you all right . . .?
DOROTHY	Of course I'm all right. Do you want a drink?
DORIS	I'll take a small gin and tonic.

(Dorothy starts to fix the drinks.)
Are you sure girl . . . you seem upset.
(Pause)

DOROTHY	Look . . . I've told you. Were you out or did you just come over here?

(Pause)

DORIS	I was in town getting a new bed for Randy. It's his birthday tomorrow.
DOROTHY	Honestly Doris, you and that dog.
DORIS	Dogs have birthdays too, just like the rest of us.
DOROTHY	Yes, but I mean presents.
DORIS	Well why not? It's all right for you, you've got Douglas. Randy's all we have.
DOROTHY	Is he better again?
DORIS	Not quite, but the vet says it's just his age. He's eleven tomorrow.
DOROTHY	Why go to all the expense of a new bed if he's only going to live for another year or two?
DORIS	He could live for another four or five years. I wonder how you'd feel if Charles refused to buy you a new coat, just because you're growing older.
DOROTHY	Charles refuses all my requests on instinct. If he didn't I'd think he'd got a fancy woman. I've told him that if I don't get some new clothes soon the EEC'll be declaring my wardrobe a depressed area.
DORIS:	I don't know anybody with as many clothes as you.
DOROTHY	At the rate you're going Randy'll soon have caught up with me. It was a coat and shoes a couple of weeks ago.
DORIS	Boots. Anyway, you must have more shoes than the Queen.
DOROTHY	Fashions change, you have to keep up.
DORIS	I think as you get older you need fewer clothes. Following the fashions is all right for the younger ones.
DOROTHY	I'm not giving up on life yet. I like to keep reasonably in touch. Not that anyone in this house notices what I wear

43

	mind you. I bought these black spotted tights for tonight and Charles thought they were seconds.
DORIS	John likes me to dress quietly.
DOROTHY	I don't make much noise when I'd doing it. What about another drink?
DORIS	No thanks. Goodness, have you finished that one already?
DOROTHY	I'll have another. Are you sure you wouldn't like topped up?
DORIS	I've plenty, especially when I'm driving.
DOROTHY	I suppose it wouldn't look too good to be drunk in charge of a dog's bed.
DORIS	Will there be drink at this tonight?
DOROTHY	Yes. It should be fun. We'd a row about it this morning. Charles was on his high horse, lecturing me on how to behave.
DORIS	I always make it a rule never to fight with John in the mornings. Not that we ever fight that much anyway. When a man goes out to his work in the mornings you're never sure . . . especially nowadays. Are you and Charles fighting a lot?
DOROTHY	Three times a day after meals.
DORIS	It doesn't do to be always at it.
DOROTHY	We're not always at it, I wish to God we were. We're never at it, that's half the trouble.
DORIS	You know what I mean girl. You never know what's round the next corner. Look at Wilma Purdy.
DOROTHY	Who's Wilma Purdy?
DORIS	Wilma, sure we went to school together. She was Thompson to her own name.
DOROTHY	Oh that Wilma. The Forces' Sweetheart. What's she up to now, living in sin with a vicar?
DORIS	She was buried last Thursday. I got the shock of my life.
DOROTHY	It must have been a bit of a shock to her too . . . sorry.
DORIS	She was the same age as me. Our birthdays were within a week of each other. Dead and buried. I met her Lilly in town on Saturday. I couldn't believe it. "You're joking" says I. Apparently she went in last summer and got it all taken away. Cancer. Poor Wilma. I remember she stole my first boyfriend . . . Peter McCann.
DOROTHY	Peter McCann . . . old Moonface . . . a pimple for every day of the year . . . and a boil for every leap year. Stealing him was like taking mumps from you.
DORIS	He was a nice boy, well mannered. He'd beautiful fingernails. I always hated boys who bit their nails.
DOROTHY	I don't know, at least they didn't cut themselves when they picked their noses.

44

	(She enjoys Doris' disapproval.)
	Do you remember Charles when we were going together?
DORIS	He used to tease me all the time.
DOROTHY	Tease you, he despised you. He used to say to me, 'If you crossed your granny with your great granny, you'd get your Doris."
	(Pause)
	When I think . . . I used to live for every date then. He was so full of life . . . never a dull moment. Now he acts like somebody who keeps ulcers as pets.
DORIS	I didn't know he didn't like me. Mind you I wasn't dying about him either. He was too full of himself.
DOROTHY	He'd reason to be . . . then. He likes you now all right.
DORIS	How did I win his approval?
DOROTHY:	You're Mammy Bear, straight up the middle. Middle-aged, middle-class, middle-of-the-road. You didn't grow old, you just stayed old.
DORIS	I've always taken life more seriously than you.
DOROTHY	Why take life seriously? You could end up like poor old Wilma. Mind you she got good mileage out of it before they took it away.
DORIS	I think there's a cruel streak in you girl.
DOROTHY	I'm desperate, not cruel. If they were to bury me next Thursday, I wouldn't even protest that I was still alive.
	(Pause)
	Tell me, do you and John still make love?
DORIS	What on earth sort of a question's that?
DOROTHY	At our age I suppose it's a statistical one.
DORIS	It's not the sort of thing I discuss.
DOROTHY	Neither do we. Charles makes me feel like a nympho on an overtime ban. I suppose it's our background. Did dad ever tell you the facts of life?
DORIS	No, but then he probably thought I'd never need to know them.
DOROTHY	He took me aside at our reception, just as we were getting ready to leave on our honeymoon. He lit his pipe, on the twenty-third match, drew himself up, blushing to his boots and said, "Well girl, you've made your bed, now you're going to have to lie in it."
	(Pause)
DORIS	How's Douglas?
DOROTHY:	Isle-of-Man, or son of Charles? I see him at breakfast occasionally. He just rushed straight out this morning. I suppose he heard us fighting. Sometimes I manage to stay awake late enough to catch him at supper. The men in my life keep themselves very busy. I think Douglas

	would die sooner than spend an evening alone with me.
DORIS	I suppose with all his Union business. . .?
DOROTHY	He's grateful for that. I know nothing about it, so he can easily fob me off about meetings. . .
DORIS	The young like their independence.
DOROTHY	Oh Doris shut up. I sometimes wonder if mother really died, or if you just absorbed her.
DORIS	I'm just pointing out . . . they have to live their own lives.
DOROTHY	I wonder how you'd feel if Randy was out chasing a different bitch every night of the week. Or going to kennel meetings all the time. At least you can shut the door on a dog. *(Pause)* I wish to God I hadn't interfered between him and Sonia Montgomery. *(She goes and fixes herself another drink.)* Do you want topped up?
DORIS	No I'm fine, I've still got tons left.
DOROTHY	Why don't you drink the stuff and stop torturing it? *(Pause)* Tell me, what do you and John do at nights?
DORIS	Well . . . I suppose . . . we watch television. He does the dinner dishes and . . . we watch television.
DOROTHY	Do you ever talk? I mean do you ever turn the television off and just sit and talk?
DORIS	Yes . . . well no . . . it depends, I mean there's not always a lot to say. We talk about Randy sometimes.
DOROTHY	I thought I was missing something. *(Pause)*
DORIS	We're happy. I think people with children have more to talk about.
DOROTHY	At least you're together . . . if there was anything to say, you wouldn't have to shout. *(Pause)* I'd love to sit for a whole evening . . . just the three of us and talk. What sort of life am I leading if that's a luxury? I live in silences. I have rows just to get somebody to talk to me. Charles is . . . running a business, running a football fan club, running a commentary on all I do, trying to run my life . . . He's a very busy man.
DORIS	I've never seen you like this before girl. You're in a very funny mood.
DOROTHY	Hilarious, I laugh 'till it hurts. *(Pause)* Sometimes I think of leaving him . . .
DORIS	Leaving! Why? Where would you go?

46

DOROTHY	I could find another man . . .
	(Looks towards the telephone.)
	Other men still find me attractive.
DORIS	What would Douglas do if you left?
DOROTHY	Douglas! I've invested over twenty years of love in Douglas. Now I've virtually to beg for a kind word. I don't think he's ever forgiven me for Sonia. Then he's also caught up in the middle of all this. It isn't fair on him.
DORIS	When did all this start?
DOROTHY	As soon as we hit the top. I often think that hill just represents our whole life together. We climbed it together and it was marvellous . . . the whole way up. Every night he'd sit for hours, telling me his problems, and his plans. But everything just changed when we reached the top.
	(Pause, She goes to gaze out front, down the hill.)
	He changed so much. When my old friends used to come up he threatened to call the corporation to decontaminate the streets. It was all right at first. The neighbours thought they were the cleaning ladies. I brought it on myself I suppose. Mrs. Bowden was in one morning when Elsie Chambers was here. You should have seen her face when Elsie sat down with us for a cup of tea. "Well Mrs. Chambers, what is your husband?" "He's a lazy shite who sits on his arse all day looking for work." When Charles came in I could hardly tell him for laughing.
	(Pause)
	I've hardly laughed since. That was the end of my friends visiting here. They thought it was me getting stuck up. Now I'm really stuck up . . . up here on top of this hill.
	(She takes another drink.)
DORIS	Go easy on that stuff girl. It never solved anybody's problems. Have you ever thought of doing a wee part time job?
DOROTHY	What for? I've this house and plenty of money. I'm not supposed to have any other needs. They don't listen to me Doris. They don't see the problem therefore it doesn't exist.
DORIS	You should get yourself a wee dog. They're great company. I don't know what I'd do without Randy. I often just sit and talk away to him. Maybe he doesn't understand what I'm saying, but at least he listens. If you'd a nice dog you could go out for a bit of a walk every morning.

47

DOROTHY	I'd be tempted to get a big dog and feed it on raw meat. Then I could always starve it for a day or two and it might eat him. *(They both laugh.)* *(Pause)* *(Noise of door opening. Charles enters.)*
CHARLES	Ah, hello Doris.
DORIS	Hello Charles, how are you?
CHARLES	Oh, mustn't complain. *(Pause)*
DOROTHY	Hello Charles. I'm your wife, but you probably know me better as Doris' sister. *(Pause. She sips at her drink.)* Wilma Purdy's dead.
CHARLES	Is she . . .
DOROTHY	Well I hope so . . . they've burried her. You knew her. You knew Wilma didn't you?
CHARLES	I can't say . . .
DOROTHY	Thompson as she was. She had it all taken away . . . cancer.
CHARLES	Well . . . I'm sorry to hear that . . . whoever she was.
DOROTHY	I thought you would be. *(To Doris)* He's so sensitive and sympathetic. I suppose if you handle bricks all day you get like that. You realise that houses are just brick boxes, but that people need people. *(Pause)* I know that if I had it all taken away Charles would be very sympathetic . . . as soon as he was told.
CHARLES	I see that you two have been having a wee quiet drink.
DORIS	I'd just the one small one.
DOROTHY	So had I. Why don't you pour yourself one . . . there's some vinegar in the working kitchen. *(Pause)*
CHARLES	How's John, Doris?
DORIS	He's the very best.
CHARLES	Randy?
DOROTHY	She should be so luck.
DORIS	He's not too bad, up and down you know.
DOROTHY	Let's stick to tried and tested methods I always say.
DORIS	I was out buying him a new bed today. It's a surprise, for his birthday. You should have seen the look on his face today. He couldn't understand why he couldn't come with me. *(Pause)* Yes . . . well . . . he sleeps more now.

DOROTHY	Don't we all. I was telling Doris that when we were going together you despised her.
CHARLES	Going together . . . that's over twenty years now.
DOROTHY	Well over it, but Doris remembers. She thought you were only teasing.
CHARLES	But I'm sure I was. I never hated Doris.
DOROTHY	I remember you saying once that she must have had the change of life when other girls were having their first period.
CHARLES	Now wait a minute Doris . . . I don't even remember what I said all those years ago, but I'm sure I wouldn't have said anything like that. Look . . . you shouldn't listen to anything she says . . . I mean she's talking about over twenty years ago.
DORIS	I used to think you were teasing . . .
CHARLES	I was . . . I was . . .
DOROTHY	How do you know if you don't remember what you said?
CHARLES	Because I liked Doris . . . I liked you . . . *(Pause)* You were quiet, a bit old fashioned . . . not like your big sister.
DOROTHY	Dead from the knickers to the knees you said.
CHARLES	Now look here you . . .
DORIS	It's all right Charles. I never liked you either. I always thought you were big headed. *(Douglas enters.)*
DOUGLAS	Hello Auntie Doris.
DORIS	Hello Douglas. *(Pause)* I think I'd better go.
CHARLES	Dorothy . . . you've hurt Doris' feelings.
DORIS	No. I'm all right.
DOROTHY	If she lived with you two she'd be like me, a walking wound. *(She drains her glass.)* It's time I got the tea . . . will you stay for a bit Doris?
DORIS	No, I'll have to go and get something ready for John.
DOROTHY	Thanks for coming over. I'll give you a ring tomorrow.
DORIS	Right . . . *(Dorothy goes.)* I've never seen her so depressed Charles.
CHARLES	She's not depressed, she's . . .
DORIS	No, she's depressed. You need to talk. I thought she had it all. I thought she was happy. I'm the one had to buy a dog.

CHARLES	All that was totally uncalled for. How do I know what I said twenty years ago. When you're young . . .
DORIS	I'm more worried about her than wounded by what she said.
	(The phone rings. Charles goes to answer it.)
CHARLES	Hello . . . hello . . . bloody think.
	(Putting down the receiver.)
	Must have been a wrong number or something.
DORIS	There was a wrong number earlier.
CHARLES	I'll have to get in touch with the GPO, that's all the time that's happening.
DORIS	You wouldn't know what's going on. Apparently the army has nearly everybody's phone tapped.
CHARLES	You'd never know, sure this whole place is mad.
DORIS	You'd be as well leaving a light on when you go out tonight. There's been a lot of breaking and entering around our way.
CHARLES	Sure it's the same all over. There was an old woman punched and kicked to death the other week, when her house was broken into. That was just up around the corner. These troubles are a great excuse for every bloody crook in the country. Sure we have to leave dogs on the site at night. I know what I'd do to them if I ever got my hands on them. The courts are far too soft. I'ts a good slap round the head half of them need.
DORIS	You're right there . . . but it's time I wasn't here. See and have a good time tonight. You'll have to call round Douglas. Your Uncle John's always asking about you.
DOUGLAS	I'll do that . . . cherrio Aunt Doris.
	(She goes and Charles leaves her to the door.
	When he returns he's angry.)
CHARLES	Christ, that was some bloody exhibition. One of these days I'll choke that woman. Even Doris is blaming me. Asking me to be gentle with her. I'll bloody depression her.
DOUGLAS	What were you two on about this morning?
CHARLES	I was bloody well warning her to behave herself tonight and not to be getting drunk.
DOUGLAS	It worked . . . she's got drunk this afternoon instead.
CHARLES	She should see a doctor, a psychiatrist. This is getting out of hand.
DOUGLAS	She was crying when I came down. Don't think she can't be hurt.
CHARLES	So you're blaming me?

50

DOUGLAS	No . . . I'm not blaming you. I just think . . .
CHARLES	Listen son, Christ I've tried. I built this place for her. I dug the foundations myself . . .
DOUGLAS	All right Dad, I know.
CHARLES	You seem to be accusing me son.
DOUGLAS	I'm not accusing you . . .
CHARLES	As soon as I walked in through that door she started. She got stuck into me in front of Doris. Then she turned on her as well.
DOUGLAS	Maybe that's because you're always throwing Doris up to her.
CHARLES	What on earth's she going to be like tonight in front of all those people?
DOUGLAS	I don't care about tonight. I don't even care about those people.
CHARLES	It's all very well being sympathetic to her son . . .
DOUGLAS	Dad, we're talking about my mother . . . your wife. *(Pause)*
CHARLES	We're also talking about a woman with a drink problem.
DOUGLAS	Her only problem is that she can't drink. Two drinks and she's almost on her ear. I think we're the problem. *(Dorothy enters.)*
DOROTHY	The tea's on the table, if you two want to wash your hands. *(Charles goes.)* Douglas, I'm sorry about Sonia.
DOUGLAS	Sonia! That was years ago.
DOROTHY	I thought I was doing the best for both of you.
DOUGLAS	If you hadn't interfered we'd probably have broken up even sooner than we did.
DOROTHY	You used to come here all the time. I liked her . . . I just thought you were getting too serious too soon. You still hate me for it, don't you?
DOUGLAS	Mum, I don't know what you're talking about . . . Sonia's over . . . done with, a long time ago.
DOROTHY	I just wanted you to know that I'm sorry . . . *(As she moves towards him he moves away.)*
DOUGLAS	I'd better . . . *(He goes.)*

FADE

SCENE 2

THE DARKENED LIVING ROOM AS THEY
RETURN FROM THE FUNCTION.

Dorothy enters. She switches on the cassette, Don Williams singing, "Don't You Believe". She kicks off her shoes and dances over to the drinks cabinet. Charles enters. (Followed a few minutes later by Douglas.) and glares at her while she pours herself a drink. He can barely contain himself as he marches across and stabs off the cassette.

CHARLES	We've had enough bloody cowboys for one night. *(Pause)* Have you not had enough bloody drink for one night?
DOROTHY	Of course I have. This is tomorrow's drinking I'm starting now.
CHARLES	I'm going to put a new lock on that cabinet and hide the key.
DOROTHY	Go to bed. The big long face on you. Your chin hasn't left your chest all night.
CHARLES	I was ashamed to hold my chin up with the antics of you. I'm sick talking to you about the way you carry on.
DOROTHY	I don't "carry on" as you call it, I enjoy myself.
CHARLES	You make a bloody fool of yourself. What about us? How do you think that wee lad feels the way you . . . flaunt yourself?
DOROTHY	The "wee lad's" a bit like yourself. You looked like a pair of clairvoyants at the launching of the Titanic.
CHARLES	If you could have seen yourself tonight, sprawled out on that floor, your dress near over your head, it was disgustin'.
DOROTHY	Do you know something Charlie Boy . . .
CHARLES	Don't call me that.
DOROTHY	You're dead from the neck up, and from the midriff down. The only part of you that really operates is your lungs . . . where all that hot air comes from.
CHARLES	You were the only woman of your age on that floor tonight.
DOROTHY	Bully for me, maybe I was the only one who could dance . . .
CHARLES	Dance! Is that what you call it, sure you kept falling all

52

	over the place. You made a complete ass of yourself.
DOROTHY	Here's to asses. Mine was touched a few times tonight. I think some of those fellas must have been faith healers.
CHARLES	What the hell sort of a way's that to talk in front of your son, you drunken bitch.
DOUGLAS	Dad, don't get yourself worked up on my account, Mum, I think you did go a bit too far tonight.
DOROTHY	Which bit? You know you should get up on your da's shoulder.
DOUGLAS	Listen mum, I have to go back in there and listen to those fellas talking about you.
DOROTHY	And what'll they say about me Douglas?
CHARLES	They'll say you're mutton dressed as lamb.
DOROTHY	Surely with the benefit of a university education they'll be a bit more original than that. That's the sort of thing you hear on building sites. Tell me what they'll say Douglas?
DOUGLAS	Mum . . . they'll just talk about you . . . about the way you were getting on.
DOROTHY	I see . . . about me dancing and having fun.
CHARLES	About you making a right bloody edjit of yourself, polishing the floor with the arse of your knickers.
DOROTHY	Careful Charlie Boy, now you're using words from your working class background. The Captain of the Golf Club might just be passing.
CHARLES	What's wrong with trying to improve yourself?
DOROTHY	That depends on the price you pay to do it. *(She drains her glass and starts to pour herself another.)*
CHARLES	You've had enough of that stuff. *(She drinks as he moves towards her, intent on taking the drink from her.)*
DOROTHY	Bugger off Charlie Boy.
CHARLES	I said you've had enough.
DOROTHY	Well here then you have this . . . *(She throws the drink in his face and moves to confront Douglas. Charles makes to go for her, thinks better of it, and begins wiping himself with a glasscloth.)*
CHARLES	Go'n you drunken bitch.
DOROTHY	What are your friends going to say about me Douglas?
DOUGLAS	Mum you're drunk.
DOROTHY	Yes, I am a bit, but not as much as you think. Will they say I've got nice legs Douglas? Will they? *(She pulls up her dress.)* Will they say I've got nice legs and a nice bum?
DOUGLAS	Cut it out mum, will you? *(She unbuttons the top of her dress.)*

DOROTHY	What about my breasts Douglas? Will they say I've got lovely breasts? Look . . . look at them. What will they call them, tits . . . or knockers?
CHARLES	For Christ's sake woman . . . quit that filthy talk . . . stop that exhibition in front of the lad.
DOROTHY	Is that what they'll say Douglas, is it? Will they say I'm a good looking woman, will they?
DOUGLAS	For God's sake mum.
DOROTHY	No son, no. Not for God's sake. For my sake. Just look at me once or twice and see more than your cook, your laundry woman, your cleaner. *(Pause)*
CHARLES	Cover yourself up, have you no shame? Have you not caused that lad enough embarrassment for one night? I saw one of them . . . boys . . . with his hand on you.
DOROTHY	Yes, unfortunately he didn't mean it. He stumbled.
CHARLES	Stumbled!
DOROTHY	He stumbled and his hand touched my breast.
CHARLES	He squeezed it, I bloody saw him. *(Dorothy's anger has gone now.)*
DOROTHY	Yes I suppose he did. I'm flattered that he found it big enough to hang onto . . . but he was drunk.
CHARLES	You're disgustin', bloody disgustin'. That's your son there you know. *(Pause)*
DOROTHY	You didn't even notice me tonight, did you?
CHARLES	Isn't that what I'm saying, you made damned sure everybody noticed you.
DOROTHY	I wanted you to be proud of me. The trouble I went to. I spent hours getting ready, hours. I was the best looking . . . mature . . . woman in the place, and you didn't even notice. *(She sits, suddenly, weary.)*
CHARLES	I don't think many people in there would have thought you were a mature woman. It's the last time though. There'll be no more functions for you until you learn to behave with a bit of dignity.
DOROTHY	So I'm going to be confined to my purpose built prison again.
CHARLES	You should be bloody grateful.
DOROTHY	Oh I am, I am. I've got my wonderful panoramic view across Belfast Lough. I can see the smoke and flames from explosions six miles away. What'll I do when the troubles are over? I'll have to go back to watching telly.
CHARLES	I've worked hard for what we have.
DOROTHY	I don't think you realise just how little we have.

CHARLES	What's that supposed to mean?
DOROTHY	I mean you've got labourers to mix your cement. You've got bricklayers to lay your bricks. I'm just like one of them. I'm just one of the people who works for you. Douglas, you're studying all these things, surely you can tell him what I'm talking about.
CHARLES	You're talking about people falling against your breasts and touching your bum. That's what you're talking about . . . flirting, leading people on. You've a right brass neck expecting me to just sit back and take all that.
DOROTHY	No wonder you're a builder you've got all the sensitivity of a brick.
CHARLES	I'm proud to be a builder. You wouldn't be sitting here today if I wasn't successful.
DOROTHY	So you keep telling me. People would think you didn't live here to listen to you talking. It's your house too.
CHARLES	It was built for you. You always moaned about a proper place, now you've got your proper place and you're still not content.
DOROTHY	This isn't my home, this is a prison. You put me up here among your new fancy friends, and then you drove my friends away.
CHARLES	Your friends . . . scum from the slums.
DOROTHY	And what are you?
CHARLES	I've pulled myself up out of all that . . . I'm up here now looking down on all that. I'm finished with it, and with them.
DOROTHY	I wish I was back down there. At least I could have a laugh and enjoy myself. I didn't have to clear every remark with the captain of the golf club. You shouldn't forget your background.
CHARLES:	I can't forget it. I've got you as a permanent reminder. Your "friends" used to crawl up here with their dirty, unwashed bodies, and their stinking clothes, clutching grubby packets of cheap biscuits, and you fed them up on best steak . . . aye and gin. That's your big trouble, you just don't know how to behave. As soon as you get a couple of drinks you start . . . you wear your common background as if it were a badge.
DOROTHY	You should take a good look around at your high-class friends. They're not above trying to look up my clothes or the occasional pat on the bum.
CHARLES	Who did?
DOROTHY	Never you mind who . . . they never get too grand to grope.
CHARLES	You must have imagined it.

55

DOROTHY	No I did not imagine it.
	(Charles switches off at this point.)
	Your friends down there didn't paw over me the way your friends up here do. Creeps, the whole damned lot of them. You've only to look at them to know what they are. Sure they smell like chemist's shops. How many shipyard labourers did you count up there tonight?
DOUGLAS	Mum, give it a rest . . . please.
	(Long pause.)
DOROTHY	I try to look my best so's I'll not let you down. So that you'll notice me, and be proud of me. What thanks or encouragement do I ever get? I'm accused of looking like a whin bush posing as a Spring flower.
	(Pause)
	(She rises.)
DOROTHY	I'm going to bed.
	(Charles and Douglas just gaze sullenly at the floor.)
	Can I kiss my son goodnight, or would that be attempted incest?
CHARLES	Go to bed and stop your blethering woman.
DOROTHY	Douglas?
DOUGLAS	Just go to bed mum, will you?
DOROTHY	Just a goodnight kiss?
DOUGLAS	For Christ's sake mum, will you grow up? You never want a kiss unless you've had a skinful.
DOROTHY	I always want a kiss, but I'm afraid to ask unless I've had a skinful.
DOUGLAS	Look mum . . .
DOROTHY	Never mind "look mum". I'm getting really sick of it. Look mum, look mum. Look at the way she behaves, and she behaves, and she behaves. Well I'm not other people. I'm not anyone else, I'm me. ME. It's time I was treated like someone in this house. Some night I'll walk out through that door and you'll never see me again. I'm sick of it. You two take yourselves off at weekends and I'm left here. Do you know what's going on in this place? Anything could happen to me, but do you two care? Then when I do get out I'm told not to talk to people, not to smile at people, not to laught or have fun. I'm not allowed to have any life at all.
	(Long pause.)
	(Charles takes a notebook from his pocket and turns to Douglas.)
CHARLES	As I was saying earlier, I'll go and see about berths. We don't want to miss a night's sleep on the boat.
DOUGLAS	Do you not think we're wasting money? Half of them

	never use the berths anyway.
CHARLES	I think we'll bring that up and insist on them using them.
DOUGLAS	Do you not think it would be better taking the names of those who really want one, let the others please themselves?
DOROTHY	Douglas? *(Pause)* Douglas?
DOUGLAS	I thought you were going to bed?
DOROTHY	You bastard . . .
CHARLES	Here, cut that out.
DOROTHY	You're as bad as him.
CHARLES	We're going away on Friday and you'll have the place to yourself all weekend. You can drink your fill and play your cowboy records all night if you like.
DOUGLAS	Is Bobbie Spence going?
CHARLES	He'll let me know. *(Dorothy goes on her knees in front of Douglas, to gain his attention.)*
DOROTHY	Douglas . . . I'm talking to you son. Listen to me, it's important.
DOUGLAS	It can't be that important if you have to be drunk before you say it.
DOROTHY	I'm not drunk son. I'm sober now. I know what I'm saying . . .
CHARLES	Look, you can have the cowboys and gin all to yourself all weekend.
DOROTHY	For Christ's sake Charles, let me talk.
CHARLES	If I knew how to stop you I'd have done it twenty years ago.
DOROTHY	Please Charles, please. *(Pause)* Listen to me, both of you listen to me. *(Pause)* Look . . . I love you two. I love you and I want to be loved. All I want . . . all I want . . . *(Douglas rises.)*
DOUGLAS	Tell us in the morning mum. Do you fancy some coffee dad?
CHARLES	Aye, that would be nice. *(Charles nods in Dorothy's direction. She stands, looking as if she's been hit.)*
DOUGLAS	Would you like some coffee mum? *(She looks at him as if she doesn't understand what he's said. Then she turns away.)*

57

DOROTHY	I'm going to bed.
	(She goes.)
	(Pause.)
	(Douglas sits again.)
	(Pause)
DOUGLAS	I can't stand it when she starts all that love stuff . . . then the tears and the kissing. In the morning she's too embarrassed even to speak.
CHARLES	She's getting worse, she really is. I mean that display tonight . . . it was disgustin'. I've never seen her like that in my life.
DOUGLAS	She apologised to me about Sonia this afternoon. Just out of the blue. As if it had been preying on her mind.
	(Pause)
	I saw Stephen there tonight. He was in the wee back lounge, Sonia's brother. You know some of the lads really rave about mum. They think she's really something.
CHARLES	They must be sick.
DOUGLAS	Stephen Montgomery used to go on about her all the time.
CHARLES	Aye, well sure he was sick. The way he used to slip around her when he was coming in and out of here, washing the dishes for her. I think there was a wee want in that fella. There's nothing more pathetic than a woman who won't recognise she's growing old.
DOUGLAS	It must be her age . . . you know . . . the ah . . . the ah . . .
CHARLES	No, no, it's not anything like that. It's not just a recent thing . . . she just won't grow up. A female Peter bloody Pan.
	(Pause)
DOUGLAS	Do you think maybe she misses her old friends from the street?
CHARLES	Old friends! Those people are nobody's friends. I had to fight to get away from those people, and then I had to fight to get her away. She wasn't their friend, she was their meal ticket. No son, them's the sort of people you leave behind if you ever want to make anything of yourself.
	(He checks his watch.)
	It's time I was in my own bed.
DOUGLAS	What about the coffee?
CHARLES	No, not now son, it's too late. Make yourself a cup and take it in with you. Goodnight.
DOUGLAS	Dad . . . Look, when we get back . . . I think we should talk. I'm not blaming anybody, but I think we should spend more time with her.
CHARLES	I told you this afternoon son, she needs a doctor . . .

DOUGLAS	No dad, no . . . she needs us. I'm not blaming you, honest. It's me too. I just can't take her when she's been drinking, but if we can get her . . . if we can talk. *(Pause)*
CHARLES	Maybe you're right . . . maybe . . . we'll talk about it . . . goodnight.
DOUGLAS	Goodnight dad.

FADE

SCENE 3

AS BEFORE.
Charles and Douglas are away for the weekend. As lights go up Dorothy is on the telephone. A book she was reading is on the table open.

DOROTHY   Yes . . . Yes . . . I've told you Doris. I don't know who
it was . . . he didn't say . . . he just asked for Charles,
I told him Charles was away, then he asked for Douglas
. . . pardon? . . . Well I don't know . . . I told him they
were away together . . . Doris . . . Doris . . . Charles is a
businessman, I take dozens of calls for him . . . What?
. . . yes . . . The doors are all locked . . . and the windows
are secure . . . yes. Listen, the SAS are dug in on the
front lawn, the navy are standing by in the Lough, and
the RAF are flying over at ten minute intervals . . . yes,
yes . . . I know you are love . . . Don't fuss, everything's
fine. Right . . . yes . . . look, I'll probably be in bed
before you're home . . . it's habit, years of escaping
from Match of the Day . . . all right . . . Sunday morning,
but not before nine . . . I won't . . . promise, bye, bye,
. . . yes . . . right . . . bye . . . bye . . .
(She replaces the receiver, sticking her tongue out at it.
Picks up the photograph of Charles.)
You old bastard. I can just hear you, "Doris, give her a
ring everytime you think she's putting the glass to her
lips." I suppose you think I'll give up in frustration. And
her, "Now Dorothy, you know Charles wouldn't talk
about you behind your back." It's so long since you
noticed me Charlie Boy that you don't know whether
I've got breasts or humps. Well screw you, I'll not
disappoint you.
(She replaces the photograph, face down, and fixes
herself a drink.)

59

I suppose it'll be closed circuit television next. I hope your team loses by an own goal, and that the ball is kicked into the crowd and knocks your head off.

(Pause)

(She returns to her seat. The doorbell rings. She lifts her head and listens, surprised. It rings again. She puts down the book. Rises, touches up her hair, straightens herself and goes out. Muffled voices, she returns with Stephen.

STEPHEN	How'd you know it was me?
DOROTHY	We've a very crafty wee spy hole.
STEPHEN	I didn't notice it.
DOROTHY	I've told you, it's a crafty wee one. You'd never notice it.
STEPHEN	I wondered at you just opening the door like.
STEPHEN	Don't you worry, I don't take any risks, especially these days. So, what are you doing away up here at this late hour?
STEPHEN	I was wanting to see Douglas.
DOROTHY	Well I didn't for a moment imagine you'd come all this way to see me.
STEPHEN	I don't know . . . I wouldn't mind coming up to see you. I used to like coming up here.
DOROTHY	Anyway I'm afraid you're out of luck. Douglas has gone away for the weekend. Was it something important?
STEPHEN	It was as a matter of fact. I'm way behind with one of my projects, It has to be in for Monday and I wanted to borrow a couple of books.
DOROTHY	You came away up here to borrow books?
STEPHEN	No, no, I didn't come up just for that. I'm going with a girl, she lives just up round the corner.
DOROTHY	Maybe I know her? I don't know very many around here. Between you and me they're not all my kind of people. What do you call her?
STEPHEN	Ah no, you wouldn't know her. They've just moved in, two weeks.
DOROTHY	I see. Look, have a drink, then I can go in and have a look for the books you want. I can offer you whiskey, sherry, port, vodka, gin, or coffee if you'd prefer it?
STEPHEN	Whiskey would be fine thanks.
DOROTHY	Do you take soda?
	(He shakes his head to indicate "no". She fixes the drink and takes it to him.)
STEPHEN	Are you not going to have one?
DOROTHY	Mine's sitting over there.
	(She moves across and they sit down.)
STEPHEN	They say it's a bad sign when you sit drinking alone.
DOROTHY	It's the first I've had all night. Do you have a car?

STEPHEN	No, I don't.
DOROTHY	How will you get home? Will you get a bus at this time of the night?
STEPHEN	Too late now. I'd hoped if Douglas was here, if he had been here, that he'd have run me home.
DOROTHY	Are you joking? I wouldn't let my Douglas drive down there at this time of night. You live in one of the most dangerous areas of the city. You sat here one night and told us there'd been four bodies found in your back garden.
STEPHEN	Well not quite in the back garden. Sort of in the field at the back. And one of them was only wounded . . . although he died the next day.
DOROTHY	Anyway, Douglas isn't here.
STEPHEN	Is Mr. Williams in?
DOROTHY	Mr. Williams?
STEPHEN	Mr. Williams . . . your husband.
DOROTHY	Yes, yes of course . . . well not in, not exactly in. He's out . . . but he'll be back soon. In fact I thought you were him.
STEPHEN	No.
DOROTHY	Pardon?
STEPHEN	I said, no, I wasn't him.
DOROTHY	No. Well of course you weren't.
STEPHEN	Will he be much later? Maybe he'll run me home.
DOROTHY	He will not. Look, why don't you ring for a taxi?
STEPHEN	Ah too dangerous. You never know who these taxi drivers are. As soon as they hear where you want to go they know what you are. Know what I mean? You drive, don't you?
DOROTHY	You don't seriously think I'd drive you home at this time of night. Anyway I haven't driven for years. I gave Douglas my car. I must say I'm slightly surprised to see you. I didn't think Douglas and you bothered much now.
STEPHEN	Well there was a while, just after he finished seeing Sonia. I mean she was, is, my sister.
DOROTHY	I'd nothing against her, but I did think they were too young to marry. *(Pause)*
STEPHEN	You're a very goodlooking woman. *(Pause)*
DOROTHY	It's getting . . . late.
STEPHEN	It doesn't matter, you're still goodlooking.
DOROTHY	I think you'd better be going.
STEPHEN	We used to talk about you.
DOROTHY	If Charles comes in . . .

61

STEPHEN	All the boys used to talk about you.
DOROTHY	Really, all of them talk . . . about me?
STEPHEN	You were everybody's favourite older woman.
DOROTHY	What were those books?
STEPHEN	The universal Mrs. Robinson. It was a film. She was a film star.
DOROTHY	I think it would be better if you were gone before Charles gets in.
STEPHEN	You kissed me once. True. It was Rag Day. I was dressed as a pirate. I walked four miles out of my way to kiss you. You were a marvellous kisser.
DOROTHY	Was I?
STEPHEN	Great.
DOROTHY	Really?
STEPHEN	Are you still a marvellous kisser?
DOROTHY	You'd better go now, it's getting very late.
STEPHEN	Yes, it does that I've noticed. Late, later, much later. Very late. Very much later.
DOROTHY	How's Sonia, Stephen?
STEPHEN	You're nervous Mrs. Williams.
DOROTHY	Nervous! Me? Don't be absurd. Why should I be nervous?
STEPHEN	Dangerous times we're living in, and it's very quiet here, very isolated.
DOROTHY	We like it quiet. The neighbours don't keep us awake.
STEPHEN	And you don't keep the neighbours awake.
DOROTHY	We don't have parties.
STEPHEN	The neighbours wouldn't hear you.
DOROTHY	We live quietly.
STEPHEN	You're rich enough to be out of screaming distance. I mean, if you screamed the neighbours wouldn't hear you.
DOROTHY	Why would I scream?
STEPHEN	Don't know. Maybe cut yourself shaving, panic at the sight of blood.
DOROTHY	Would you go now, please? Please. It's late and I'm tired.
STEPHEN	What about Mr. Williams?
DOROTHY	He has a key.
STEPHEN	A key . . . a doorkey?
DOROTHY	Yes.
STEPHEN	Seems a bit silly, him having a doorkey. I mean you had the door bolted.
DOROTHY	I know I had, I always bolt the door.
STEPHEN	What good's his key if you've the door bolted? *(Long pause.)* You're a lovely woman. You really work at it, don't you?

DOROTHY	I like to look my best . . . it makes me feel better. Look Stephen . . . you really . . .
STEPHEN	Did you know that Douglas used to kiss Sonia?
DOROTHY	Well, they were virtually engaged.
STEPHEN	And then you stopped it.
DOROTHY	I did it for both their sakes. I just wanted them to wait a while.
STEPHEN	They used to sleep together . . . here . . . when you were away. *(Pause)* You're not surprised?
DOROTHY	I suppose it's the way things are nowadays . . . I never thought about it.
STEPHEN	I stayed here one weekend when you were away. Your mother was sick or something. My girlfriend was with me and we slept in there.
DOROTHY	That's my room.
STEPHEN	I know, the master bedroom. Separate beds. We used your bed. I knew it by the smell. We did it twice . . . and I pretended it was you. *(She rises.)*
DOROTHY	How dare you talk to me like that. Now will you please get out of my house? You can see Douglas yourself next week and ask him about the books.
STEPHEN	You're a lovely woman. All the blokes think you're really nice looking. A woman at your age. I think it's great.
DOROTHY	Will you get out of here.
STEPHEN	If you tried to throw me out we could have a quare wrestle. I'd enjoy that.
DOROTHY	Come on now, don't be silly. If Charles comes in you're only going to get yourself into trouble.
STEPHEN	If my old woman looked like you I'd stay home and protect her. Belfast's a dangerous place. Do you know the murder rate's on the increase? Of course the suicide rate's fallen. I read it's the safest place in the world to have a heart attack in. This special ambulance they have. I reckon the Yanks'll soon be coming over to have their heart attacks, the way they do to have their babies.
DOROTHY	Stephen, please go home. I'll pay for a taxi for you.
STEPHEN	You don't sleep with your husband.
DOROTHY	Stephen . . .
STEPHEN	I like to hear you saying my name. I've really fancied you for years, do you know that? If you don't sleep with your husband . . . why do you always try to look so good?
DOROTHY	I've had enough of this. Are you going to leave, before I call the police?

63

	(She moves towards the phone.)
STEPHEN	All right . . . I'm sorry, it's this . . . I've had a lot tonight.
	(He finishes his drink.)
	Look I'm really sorry Mrs. Williams. Can I use your toilet and then I'll go?
DOROTHY	It's at the end of the hall.
STEPHEN	I remember . . . I didn't mean to frighten you.
DOROTHY	I'm not frightened.
STEPHEN	I didn't mean to annoy you.
DOROTHY	I'm not annoyed. For God's sake, I'm just very tired.
STEPHEN	Right, I'll go to the toilet.
DOROTHY	Will I call a taxi for you?
STEPHEN	No . . . no taxi.
DOROTHY	But how are you going to get home at this time of the night?
STEPHEN	I'll ah . . . I'll go back round to the girlfriend's house. I'll be all right, don't worry.
	(He goes pulling the living-room door shut behind him. Dorothy goes to the kitchen and fetches a large carving knife. She slips it under magazines on the coffee table. She sits nervously on the edge of the settee.)
	(Pause)
	(The front door bangs . . . she jumps terrified.)
	(Pause . . . Silence)
DOROTHY	Stephen? Stephen?
	(She rises slowly.)
	Stephen, are you there?
	(Silence. She looks nervously around the room, then moves slowly to the door. Gingerly puts her hand on the door handle.)
	Stephen?
	(Pulls the door open quickly. After a long pause she moves out into the hall.)
	Stephen . . . are you there?
	(She is heard bolting the door. Comes quickly in and grabs the telephone. Dials. Works frantically at the phone, before she realises it is dead.)
	Hello . . . hello . . . oh God . . . hello . . .
	(The door opens and Andy enters. A heavily built, cruel looking individual. He bangs the door closed, Dorothy turns quickly. She opens her mouth to scream, but no sound emerges. Andy speaks in a deep gruff voice.)
ANDY	You scream missus and I'll cut your throat. Sit down there.

64

	(Dorothy makes two or three abortive attempts to speak before she manages it.)
DOROTHY	Who . . . who are you? What do you want? How did . . .
ANDY	You'd better sit down missus.
	(She sits at the end of the settee closest to the concealed knife.)
DOROTHY	Please . . . please . . . I've got money . . . and jewellery.
ANDY	Shut up missus. If I want money or jewels I'll take them. Doesn't make any difference to anything else.
DOROTHY	My husband'll be back any minute. I'm expecting him. He's on his way.
ANDY	Get me a drink.
DOROTHY	Pardon?
ANDY	A drink, are you corn beef?
	(She goes to the drinks.)
DOROTHY	What do you want?
ANDY	Vodka.
DOROTHY	What are you going to do to me?
ANDY	I'll do what I'm told.
DOROTHY	Told? By who . . . who else is here?
ANDY	I'll do what I'm told, doesn't matter to me.
DOROTHY	But why for God's sake? Why pick on me? I've never done anything on you.
ANDY	Bring me that drink and shut up missus.
	(He takes the drink with one hand and grabs her arm with the other.)
	I hope it's something we can both enjoy.
DOROTHY	You're hurting me.
ANDY	'Course I'm hurting you, it's easy. So long as you just understand how easy it is for me to hurt you, you'll not try to do anything daft.
	(He drinks. Stephen and Mike enter. Mike is a good-looking, muscular man, obviously the leader. On seeing Stephen, Dorothy's reaction is almost one of relief.)
DOROTHY	Stephen! What is this, who are these people? What's going on?
STEPHEN	This is Mike.
	(Mike approaches with his hand extended. She hesitates, he waits. When they do shake hands he exerts enough pressure to make her grimace.)
MIKE	I'm very pleased to meet you . . . Dorothy. Sit down and Stephen'll get you a drink. That's it. Stephen, get the lady a large gin.
DOROTHY	I don't . . .
MIKE	What! You don't what?
DOROTHY	No, . . . no . . . it's all right. A gin would be lovely.

STEPHEN	What about you Mike?
MIKE	I'll have milk. The old stomach's playing me up. Do you have milk Dorothy?
DOROTHY	Yes . . . it's . . .
MIKE	You sit there . . . just relax. Stephen'll get it. You look puzzled, what is it?
DOROTHY	I just thought . . . you sound . . .
MIKE	Yes, I do sound . . . don't I?
ANDY	She says her husband'll be back any minute.
MIKE	Is that a fact?
DOROTHY	He should . . . I'm expecting . . .
	(Mike jumps to his feet and faces her. She shrinks back terrified as he shouts at her.)
MIKE	Relax woman, will you? I hate frightened women. Sit up properly.
	(He pulls her to her feet.)
	Kiss me.
	(Pause)
	(She gives him a quick nervous peck.)
	I hope for your sake you can do a lot better than that. Now kiss me properly.
	(She does.)
	That's better. Now sit down and relax.
	(She does, and he sits down beside her.)
	You see Dorothy if you keep me happy you don't have to worry about a thing. These two don't count. They'll do whatever I say.
	(Pause. Stephen hands out the drinks.)
	I suppose you're wondering why we're here . . . are you?
DOROTHY	Yes . . . yes.
	(He pulls the table round towards himself. He sees the knife and holds it up.)
MIKE	I see you were planning to do your toenails.
	(He hands the knife to Stephen. He takes a heavy revolver from his pocket and places it on the table. Drinks his milk.)
	This is good milk, very good . . . cows?
DOROTHY	Pardon?
MIKE	Is it cows' milk?
DOROTHY	It's from the Co-op . . . yes, yes, I suppose it is cow's milk.
MIKE	It's very, very good.
DOROTHY	I'm glad you like it so much.
MIKE	Yes I do. Would you like to go to bed with me?
DOROTHY	Pardon?
	(He starts fingering the gun.)

MIKE	Go to bed with me. Of course you don't have to. You're not being forced to.
	(He points the gun at her.)
	You have the right to refuse, you can say no. I believe in women's lib, choice and all that stuff. You can refuse to go to bed with me. Mind you, you'd be the first woman ever to refuse to go with me. I'm not sure how I'd react to a refusal. Andy, how do you think I'd react to a refusal?
ANDY	You'd probably shoot her . . . right through the tit.
	(Andy laughs delightedly.)
MIKE	Now, now Andy. Let's not be crude. Women in Dorothy's position don't have tits. They have breasts. Stephen, how do you think I'll react if she says no?
STEPHEN	I think you might take it out on Charles and Douglas.
DOROTHY	Look please . . . this is ridiculous . . . stop it, please.
MIKE	Stephen I think you've upset the lady. Why don't you tell her why we're here. Maybe she'll see things clearer then.
	(Pause. Mike puts down the gun.)
STEPHEN	It's about Sonia . . . Dorothy. It's about my sister and your son.
DOROTHY	Sonia and Douglas broke up two years ago.
STEPHEN	Ah no, not that long ago. You might have thought it was over, but he kept seeing her.
DOROTHY	Douglas wouldn't betray my trust.
STEPHEN	Wise up Dorothy baby. Your Dougie . . .
DOROTHY	Douglas.
STEPHEN	Proper pronunciation doesn't change what he is. He's a shit, a supershit. He went on seeing her. They went on sleeping together. About eighteen months ago Sonia got pregnant.
DOROTHY	You're a liar, this is rubbish.
STEPHEN	We're talking about my sister . . .
DOROTHY	And my son.
STEPHEN	And your son, but I know my sister . . .
DOROTHY	And I know my son.
STEPHEN	Then why didn't you know what I'm telling you?
	(She jumps to her feet.)
DOROTHY	Because it's lies. I don't believe a word of it.
MIKE	Dorothy! Sit down and shut that great hole between your nose and your chin. Now just be quiet and listen, otherwise Andy'll put your skirt up over your head and tie it there. Sit.
DOROTHY	It's not true. I know it's not true.
	(She sits slowly.)
STEPHEN	Thanks Mike. Dougie . . . knocked my sister up the shoot.

67

	Then he arranged an abortion. The crank he took her to nearly killed her . . . do you hear that? She nearly died . . . and now she's been told that she can never have children . . . never. She's been ruined, and who's to blame? Your son, your wonderful Douglas. The coming young man. The high-flying president of the students' union.
DOROTHY	I don't . . . I can't believe it. Douglas wouldn't . . .
STEPHEN	Ah but Douglas bloody did. She couldn't come to you, not after the way you treated her, and your charming son wanted nothing to do with her. He dropped her like a red hot brick . . . and that's why we're here . . . *(He picks up the gun.)* revenge . . . justice.
DOROTHY	Oh my God . . . you can't . . .?
STEPHEN	If we point this gun at your Douglas and press this trigger, ther'll be a loud bang, an explosion. A little lead bullet will emerge from this end . . . and it should cause considerable damage to whichever part of Mr. Wonderful it hits. *(Mike takes the gun from Stephen and replaces it on the table.)*
MIKE	You see Andy there Dorothy? Since 1969 Andy's killed more people than Billy the Kid. We always try to encourage him to use a gun . . . but he prefers slower, messier, more painful ways. He's a craftsman, and all craftsmen like to leave their individual touch. *(Pause)* Now you should be able to understand how that young girl feels. You're a woman yourself, and a very attractive one. Everybody knows how you like to dress up and flirt with younger men.
DOROTHY	I don't flirt, I'm a happily married woman.
MIKE	I saw you the other night. I was there. Stephen got me a ticket, but we ah, we stayed in the background. We were going to hit Douglas then but seeing you . . . well, it sort of give us an idea. You were having a great time, teasing all the young fellas. That time you slipped on your arse . . . I had to hold Stephen down. Do you see what I'm saying? Now you just think about that . . . and then you think about Sonia. How would you've liked to have been ruined at her age? *(Pause)* I know Sonia . . . she's a lovely girl.
ANDY	Ruined missus.
DOROTHY	Look Stephen . . . I'm sorry . . . I'm terribly sorry about Sonia. I'll make it up to her in some way . . . I'll talk to Douglas.

68

	(Stephen and Mike roar with laughter. Andy joins in.)
MIKE	She'll talk to Douglas.
STEPHEN	She'll tell him he's been a naughty boy.
	(Mike slaps the back of Stephen's hand.)
MIKE	Naughty, naughty Douglas. You're the randiest old president since J.F.K.
	(She jumps up.)
DOROTHY	Shut up . . . shut up . . . damn you all, shut up.
	(They stop laughing. Mike punches her in the stomach and she falls down.)
MIKE	You shut up. Stephen get some more drink. Milk for me. This bitch is upsetting my stomach again. Now you listen to me Dorothy. We know you're all alone here. You thought you recognised my voice earlier and so you did. We've been talking a lot recently. How did you explain all those wrong numbers to dear old Charles? Stephen phoned you the night, and you told him Charles and Douglas were away for the weekend.
	(Pause)
	Now don't you try to treat us like fools. We didn't just walk in here the night on the off chance. This has been planned. Stephen and me have spent a fortune phoning you. You're paid for missus.
	(Pause)
	Whether you ever see Charles or Douglas again's up to you. I warned you to stay on the right side of me. You slip up again and Andy can have you for his supper. Do you get me?
DOROTHY	Yes . . . I'm sorry.
	(Mike takes a long drink of milk while Stephen fixes himself and Andy up.)
MIKE	That's better. No more screaming. No more tears. I'll decide everything. Once I make up my mind that's it. All the screaming and tears in the world won't make any difference. As a matter of fact they make things worse.
STEPHEN	What about her? *(offering drink)*
MIKE	No. I want her sober for the rest of this. You want to help Douglas, don't you Dorothy?
	(She stares at him. At the others. Back at him.)
DOROTHY	You phoned me earlier. You know Charles and Douglas are away for the weekend . . .
MIKE	You're not dumb Dorothy. We took a really good look at you the other night. That's when we got our idea. Well, credit where it's due, it's Stephen's idea. If you really want to help Douglas then there's no problem at

	all. The thing is, if we decide to wait for Douglas . . . his da's going to be with him. We'd have to fix them both, and . . . eventually . . . you. *(Pause)* You're a very attractive woman Dorothy.
STEPHEN	She's a great kisser.
MIKE	You're a sensational kisser. The way I reckon it Dorothy . . . it's either you in that bedroom, or Douglas and his da in their graves. That's the way I see it.
DOROTHY	No, no. Oh my God, please, please . . . no. *(She drops on her knees.)* I'm begging you, please . . . not that . . .
MIKE	You're not thinking straight. Nobody says "no" to me. Nobody. Now you get in there.
DOROTHY	No, no, I'd rather be shot. Shoot me if you like. *(He grabs her face.)*
MIKE	You're not as bright as I thought. We'll shoot you when we're finished if that's what you want. But let me tell you something, if you're not good in there, Charles and Douglas are dead. Do you hear me . . . dead.
DOROTHY	Please, look, I've got money . . . jewellery . . .
MIKE	You've got nothing. The only thing you've got is what we decide to leave you with. *(He takes a deep drink of his milk.)* You're starting my bloody stomach again. We're offering you what you've always wanted. You've flaunted yourself for years. You've flirted and teased. Deep down you want it. Deep down you want to be taken.
DOROTHY	It isn't true, honestly it isn't true. Stephen you tell them . . . please. You used to come in here . . . you stayed here . . . I treated you well . . . please tell them.
STEPHEN	I have told them . . . that's why we're here.
DOROTHY	Is it a crime to have pride in yourself, to be clean and well dressed?
STEPHEN	Come off it. You love all the attention you get.
DOROTHY	All right, I like to be looked at, to be admired . . .
MIKE	Lusted after?
DOROTHY	No . . . admired, just admired. I'm old enough to be your mother. Would you like anyone to do this to your mother? *(He grabs her roughly.)*
MIKE	You're not my ma. My ma's a lady. My ma's spent most of her life on her knees, cleaning for sluts like you. You're an overdressed, middle-class whore. *(He lets her go.)*
DOROTHY	I'm not middle-class, and if I'm a whore why do you want to rape me?

MIKE	Because you've been asking for it, and tonight's your lucky night. But let's get one thing straight . . . I'm not going to rape you. You're going to walk into that bedroom of your own free will. Do you understand? *(She struggles to her feet.)*
DOROTHY	Never . . . no . . . I'll never do that . . . never. *(He grabs hold of her and throws her down on the settee.)*
MIKE	All right you've made your choice. You're a very a attractive woman. But after the night you'll be known as the ugliest, childless widow in Ireland. *(Pause)* Andy . . . let's see just how good you really are. *(Andy hesitates, unsure. Then he takes a long bladed knife from his inside pocket.)*
ANDY	All right missus, you're all mine now. *(He moves slowly towards her, displaying the knife. He grabs her hair and pulls her head back.)*
STEPHEN	Hold on Andy. Mrs. Williams. Dorothy . . . for God's sake. You don't know what he's like. Once he's seen blood nothing or nobody'll stop him.
ANDY	Shut you up. She's had her chance. Get me a towel.
STEPHEN	What do you want a towel for?
ANDY	I'm not going to slash through blood. I want to make a real good mess of this one.
MIKE	Get the towel Stephen. *(Pause)* Get him the towel. We've wasted enough time trying to be nice to her. *(As Stephen goes Andy makes as if to start.)*
DOROTHY	All right I'll do it . . .
ANDY	You're too late.
MIKE	Do what?
ANDY	She's had her chance Mike.
MIKE	Hold it just a second Andy. Now what is it you want to do?
DOROTHY	I'll do what you want. *(Stephen returns with the towel.)*
MIKE	I want you to tell me what you want to do. I want you to put it into words. *(Andy grabs the towel and starts to fix it around her chest, under her chin.)*
DOROTHY	I'll go into the bedroom with you.
MIKE	Are you asking me to go to bed with you?
DOROTHY	Yes.
MIKE	Yes what?
DOROTHY	Yes . . . Mike. Yes, I'm asking you to go to bed with me.

71

MIKE	I'm not sure I want to go with you now, the notion's off me. I think it'd be much more fun to watch Andy at work.
DOROTHY	Please . . .
MIKE	I've got a name.
DOROTHY	Please Mike . . . take me into the bedroom and screw me and have done with it.
MIKE	The things women ask me to do. Do you know something Andy, you're better than expensive after-shave. Lead the way Dorothy.
	(Andy pulls the towel off her.)
ANDY	I think she'd be better sliced than screwed.
	(He laughs. As Dorothy passes, Stephen touches her bottom.)
STEPHEN	I'm second.
DOROTHY	What! No, no . . . I'm not going with you as well . . .
	(Andy points the knife at her.)
ANDY	Ah . . . and then me missus.
STEPHEN	You haven't read your Dumas, Dorothy.
	(Mike pushes her ahead of him towards the bedroom.)

FADE

MAIN INTERVAL

SCENE 4

THE SAME.
Mike and Dorothy are still in the bedroom. Stephen goes across and hovers around the bedroom door.

ANDY	Hey, cut that out.
STEPHEN	Maybe they've fallen asleep in there.
ANDY	Mike wouldn't like it. You'll get your turn.
	(Stephen comes back and sits down.)
STEPHEN	How long do you reckon he'll be?
ANDY	About nine inches.
	(Stephen laughs loudly. Andy doesn't. His mood is changed. His strong dislike of Stephen is beginning to surface.)

72

STEPHEN:	Would you really have used that knife on her?
ANDY	What do you think?
STEPHEN	Have you ever done a job like this before?
ANDY	This isn't a job, this is your idea.
STEPHEN	How many people have you killed for Mike?
ANDY	I haven't killed anybody for Mike. I've killed for . . . for reasons.
STEPHEN	But Mike's always told you who . . .
ANDY	I've told you.
STEPHEN	Why do you use a knife? If I was going to kill somebody I'd prefer to use a gun. It's not as messy.
ANDY	Messy . . . the night I went to identify my da, do you know what he was like?
	(Pause)
	He was like a big steak and kidney pie that somebody'd tramped through in their boots, and then covered in tomato sauce. There were bits of him that were never found . . . but it was the smell. He wouldn't have liked to smell like that. He might have been a drunken oul bastard, but he didn't deserve that. I don't need anybody to tell me who. I know who. I know who killed my da.
STEPHEN	I know how you feel.
ANDY	Now you know fuck all about it. To you I'm just a thick bastard with a knife. I'm one of the ones all your poncy lecturers and those two-faced politicians talk about . . . a sadistic killer . . . a homicidal maniac.
STEPHEN	I've never said that Andy.
ANDY	I have to laugh at their old crap: "Nothing can justify these sadistic killers. "What do they know about justification? How would they feel if their das had been scraped off the ground on a shovel and put in a plastic bag? I'll kill a thousand of the bastards before I'm done.
	(Pause)
STEPHEN	It would be nice to live in a place like this . . .
	(Dorothy can be heard moaning and crying.)
ANDY	We shouldn't even be here. That woman's got fuck all to do with it. It's you, you, you bloody wee pervert.
STEPHEN	You didn't have to come Andy. I mean . . .
	(Andy angrily drags him to his feet.)
ANDY	It's you, you bastard, it's your fault I'm here.
	(He throws Stephen down and starts to threaten him with the knife.)
	That woman never did nothing on me. D'you know, I reckon when we're finished here we should go down and do your ma. Your oul woman thinks she is something, just because you're a poncy wee university student. What

	would she say if she knew about this? I watch the oul bitch walking down the street. If the dog's shite was up to the window sills she wouldn't notice, her oul powdered nose is that high in the air.
STEPHEN	Be careful with that knife Andy.
ANDY	Do you fancy that, eh? Do you fancy doin' your own oul woman? What do they call that?
STEPHEN	You're going to cut me with that knife.
ANDY	What's the name of that? Doin' your oul woman. What's it called?
STEPHEN	Incest . . . look . . .
ANDY	D'you know the only reason I wouldn't do your oul woman is that the oul bitch'd probably enjoy it.
STEPHEN	For fucks sake Andy, watch that knife.
	(Andy rises.)
ANDY	Ah, if I wanted to I could cut you up into half-pound steaks.
	(Mike enters. Dorothy sobs in the bedroom.)
MIKE	Who said women don't enjoy it? She nearly devoured me. Listen to her crying for more.
	(Pause. Andy puts his knife away.)
ANDY	Go on wee man. Go and have your fun. Let her see what it's like with a bastard. You'd never get a woman any other way.
	(As Stephen goes he kicks him on the backside. Mike takes a drink.)
	Here now, you'll start your stomach again.
MIKE	Ah to hell with it. What were you and superbrain up to?
ANDY	I don't like that wee bastard . . . never did. I hope he's not going to be with us again.
MIKE	No way, it's a one-off. He knew the set-up. We couldn't have got in without him.
ANDY	We shouldn't have come in. You shouldn't have listened to him. All that crap about his Sonia. He probably made most of it up. Sure she's a mad ride anyway.
MIKE	Aye, maybe you're right. Mind you, your woman looked really good that night.
ANDY	Rape, what's that got to do with us? I want to get that wee bastard.
MIKE	Not with the knife.
ANDY	I wouldn't waste it on him. I'll just kick his shite in.
MIKE	What's wrong with you all of a sudden?
ANDY	This isn't our sort of job. If they find out we're in trouble. They'll bloody kneecap us.
MIKE	It's a one-off. They'll never know. You should have seen her at that dinner dance. She let all the young fellas get a

	grope and then moved on. A real oul tease. I just looked at her and thought, "Mrs, someday I'm going to put the bloody teasing out of your head." She's got a lovely body. People like us are all right for a quick grope when she's pissed. But for the real thing you'd have to be loaded.
ANDY	What happens if she goes to the cops?
MIKE	She wouldn't dare. I told her enough wee stories in there to keep her mouth closed for ever. When you go in there, no rough stuff. I don't want a mark on her.
	(Pause)
	Give that door a bang. If he's in there any longer he's liable to enjoy himself.
	(Andy bangs the bedroom door.)
ANDY	Right you, out of there, hurry up.
STEPHEN	I'm coming, just a minute.
ANDY	What about a big dig on the gub, just as he comes through the door?
MIKE	Leave it 'till later Andy. Let's get away from here first.
ANDY	What's the oul lad do?
MIKE	He's a builder. Built this place.
ANDY	My da was a builders labourer. Is he a big one?
MIKE	No, bungalows, conversions, small time.
ANDY	The wee men are the worst. As soon as things are tight the labourers are the first to go. The brickies are suddenly able to mix their own cement. My da used to say when there was a labourer around they wouldn't even wash their own trowels. He came in one night and said the boss had got a new cement mixer: "He toul me to work harder or I was fired." Silly oul bugger. He thought that was a great joke . . . toul it to everybody.
	(Pause)
	Hey, maybe he worked for this oul frigger, eh? I'll mix her fuckin' cement for her.
MIKE	Andy, I meant what I said, no rough stuff on her.
	(Stephen emerges as Andy reaches the door.)
ANDY	What the hell kept you?
STEPHEN	Come on, I told you I was coming . . .
	(Andy bundles him out of the way.)
	. . . you never give me much time. I don't like the mood he's in Mike. He could get nasty.
MIKE	He's all right. It's the drink. He can't do anything unless he's had a few drinks. Trouble is, once he starts drinking he starts thinking about his da . . . then he's liable to do anything.
STEPHEN	I got the whole thing about his da. I didn't think he could stand his da. Sure they were always fighting.

MIKE	That's the trouble. The night the oul lad was killed Andy gave him a hidin'. The da hit the oul woman, so Andy kicked his shite in. Then the oul fella went to the bar and . . . bang. If they hadn't had that row . . .
STEPHEN	I thought he was going to carve me up.
MIKE	Relax, just ignore him when he goes like that. I'll tell you something but, if he ever finds out there's nothin' wrong with your Sonia, you've had it.
STEPHEN	Maybe we should have done it on our own.
MIKE	If we didn't have Andy she'd have squealed the place down. We'd probably have had to choke her.
	(Stephen races across and fixes himself a drink.)
STEPHEN	Boy, she was good. You were right. She nearly raped me.
MIKE	You enjoyed it?
STEPHEN	It's the best I've had in a long time. What about you?
MIKE	Did she say anything?
STEPHEN	She just kept moaning and asking for more. She told me I was good.
MIKE	Did she say anything about me?
STEPHEN	Yes, she did . . . she ah . . .
	(Mike picks up the gun and points it at Stephen.)
	She said you were . . . ah good . . . great in fact.
MIKE	You're a lying bastard.
STEPHEN	Don't Mike, you should never point a gun at anybody.
MIKE	How are you going to shoot them if you don't point it at them?
STEPHEN	For Christ's sake Mike, first Andy and now you.
MIKE	Don't tell me you're beginning to doubt your popularity, Stephen? Did you smell anything when you were in there?
STEPHEN	Smell . . . what smell?
MIKE	Like somebody'd been sick?
STEPHEN	I never noticed . . . was it your stomach?
MIKE	She was sick, as soon as I took off my trousers. I was going to strangle her. I would have, but she wouldn't have cared. She hated it . . . and she hated me. She just cried and begged me to stop the whole time. It was lousy.
STEPHEN	She cried a bit but . . .
MIKE	Don't say anything else Stephen, otherwise I'll pull this trigger. The big lad's right. This isn't our type of thing. I shouldn't have listened to you. Fucking pervert. I hope Andy finds out it was all lies. I'll blame you. I'll say I believed you too. He'll cut your throat from ear to ear. *(Pause. He sets the gun back on the table.)*

76

STEPHEN	I'm sorry Mike. I thought she'd be great. I've been wanting to screw that woman for years. I thought she was looking for it, she was always that friendly. I've looked forward . . .
MIKE	Shut up. There's my bloody stomach starting up again. Go and get me some milk . . . hurry up.
	(Stephen goes for the milk. Mike sits hugging himself, rocking backwards and forwards to ease the pain. He gulps down the milk.)
	Christ, I'm going to die. I know it. I'm going to die. Get me some more milk.
	(Mike rises shakily and in agony staggers to the door.)
STEPHEN	Where are you going?
MIKE	The bog . . . I'm sick . . .
	(He goes.)
STEPHEN	One's a nutcase, and the other's a bloody invalid.
	(He goes and fixes himself a "shot". Andy comes in.)
ANDY	You still drinking? Here . . . where's Mike?
STEPHEN	He went to the toilet, he's not well.
	(Stephen has his eyes on the gun.)
ANDY	I told the stupid frigger not to drink anymore.
STEPHEN	I've never seen him so bad. Maybe you'd better go and check up.
	(Andy glares at him, picks up the gun and goes. Stephen gulps down his drink and moves cautiously towards the bedroom.)
	(Pause)
	(Andy comes rushing back in.)
ANDY	Stephen . . . Stephen . . . He's bad. I've never seen him this bad. I think he's dying, he's bringing up blood.
	(Andy rushes back out. Stephen follows him to the door, then he turns and picks up the phone . . . dials . . . after a few seconds remembers.)
STEPHEN	Oh Christ, the bloody phone . . .
	(Andy coming back . . .)
ANDY	What . . .?
STEPHEN	The phone, we can't get an ambulance.
ANDY	We have to get one. He's really bad. Look . . . ah . . . go next door and use the phone.
	(He hands him the gun.)
	Here take this . . . move.
STEPHEN	Are you nuts?
ANDY	Go I'm telling you.
STEPHEN	And what'll I say? "Excuse me can I use your phone? Me and my mates were just raping the woman next door and one of them's sick?"

ANDY	I'll kill you, you bastard. I'll kill you for this.
STEPHEN	It's not my fault . . .
ANDY	The whole thing's your fault. It was your idea.
STEPHEN	Look, come on Andy, he needs treatment. He could die.
ANDY	If he dies I'll kill you.
STEPHEN	Go on you great thick maniac . . . it's not my fault. *(Andy picks up Dorothy's knife that Stephen had left on the drinks cabinet.)*
ANDY	I'm going to cut your fuckin' head off for that. *(Stephen raises the gun.)*
STEPHEN	You come at me and I'll shoot . . . I'm warning you.
ANDY	You wouldn't have the guts . . . and even if you did the boys . . . *(Mike has appeared in the doorway.)*
MIKE	Andy . . . Andy . . . aaaahh . . . Andy . . .
ANDY	I'm going to get you boy, you can bet your life on that. *(He half carries, half drags Mike to the settee. Mike is writhing in agony and moaning.)* I warned him not to drink. What in the name of Jasus are we going to do?
STEPHEN	What about her?
ANDY	Can you not think about nothing else?
STEPHEN	No, not that. The car, she can drive.
ANDY	Can she?
STEPHEN	She used to have a car I'll ask her. *(He goes into the bedroom. Asking as he enters the room. Muffled voices.)* Can you drive?
ANDY	There mate, come on hold on. You'll be all right. She'll run us to the hospital. Just hold on. If he's doing anything in there I'll kill him. *(Stephen comes to the door.)*
STEPHEN	She says she'll see him in hell first.
ANDY	Oh she'll see him in hell all right . . . she'll be there to open the gates.
	(He storms into the bedroom, shouting and attacking her. She can be heard crying out in pain.)
MIKE	Stephen . . . stop him for Christ's sake . . . stop the stupid bastard before he kills her. *(Stephen, still holding the gun, goes to the bedroom door, screaming.)*
STEPHEN	Leave her alone Andy . . . leave her alone or I'll shoot Andy.

(Pause)
(Andy emerges slowly into the room. As he passes Stephen he turns and knocks the gun out of Stephen's hand. He knees him in the groin, pulls his head down and knees him repeatedly. He puts a hand across Stephen's mouth and nose and drags him to the ground. Stephen is squealing like a pig about to be slaughtered. Andy takes out his knife. He is going to slash Stephen's throat.

ANDY That's twice you've been going to shoot me. You'll never get a third chance you wee bastard.

MIKE Andy . . . A AANDY . . . !!!

(Pause)
That's enough Andy. Let him up. Come on . . . help me into the car and I'll drive it. . . .
(Pause)
(Andy rises slowly, putting the knife away and picking up the gun. Stephen is on his hands and knees. Andy turns and kicks him viciously in the stomach. Stephen collapses. Andy goes and half carries, half drags Mike out. Stephen struggles to his feet and staggers and slips after them.)
(The outside door bangs closed loudly.)
(Silence)

FADE

79

SCENE 5

Dorothy dressed in trousers and polo-neck jumper. Hair untidy. No make-up. Face bruised. Enters carrying a cup of coffee. Looks distracted. Sits, Doorbell rings. It rings again. She stirs herself. Looks in the mirror, makes no attempt to fix herself. Shuffles to the door. Comes in followed by Doris. Doris hangs her coat in the hall, but keeps her hat on. Dorothy sits.

DORIS	I rang three or four times, then I got the operator to try. She said it must be out of order. She sounded half asleep. I've told her to get a man out to look at it tomorrow. I thought I'd better call around. *(Pause)* Well, what sort . . . here girl, your face . . .
DOROTHY	I fell.
DORIS	Fell! Fell where?
DOROTHY	On my face.
DORIS	Whereabouts did you fall?
DOROTHY	Outside . . . on the path at the back.
DORIS	I see. *(Pause. Doris starts to tidy things.)* Dorothy . . . far be it for me to interfere, but I think you've got to do something about this. You're just going to have to face up to it. I know we haven't always been the best of friends, but I'll help you. We're sisters and we've got to stick together. We were just talking about you this morning. You're left far too much on your own. I'll talk to Charles and Douglas. I'ts up to them as well. I'll tell them you want help. If we all stick together love, if we all try . . . If only I'd known sooner. You should have told me. We could have been a lot closer, if it hadn't been for Charles and John not liking each other.
DOROTHY	You were always jealous of me Doris. It's not my fault you can't have children. *(Doris sits, a little taken aback.)*
DORIS	Have you had a nice weekend . . . I was nearly going to ask you over . . . but you'd probably have thought . . .
DOROTHY	I probably would. *(Suddenly jerks into life. Goes to fix herself a drink.)* Would you like a drink?

80

DORIS	No, no thanks. John doesn't . . . not on a Sunday.
DOROTHY	Go out and take a look in the back garden Doris.
DORIS	What? What for?
DOROTHY	You'll see, go on.
DORIS	You're worrying me girl . . .
DOROTHY	Damn it, will you go and look in the back garden. It isn't much to ask.
DORIS	When did you fall?
DOROTHY	On Friday night.
DORIS	Were you drunk?
DOROTHY	Will you go and look in the garden?
DORIS	We need to talk girl, we really do.
	(Dorothy waves her out. Sips her drink. Doris returns.)
	What have you been doing?
DOROTHY	I've conceded defeat to Randy.
DORIS	What have you done?
DOROTHY	A bonfire, quite common in suburban gardens. My whole wardrobe . . . coats, dresses, sexy knickers, revealing bras, see-through nighties . . .
DORIS	Why . . . for God's sake?
DOROTHY	If you've decided to sin on Sunday why not have a drink?
DORIS	I don't want any drink and I think it's time you stopped it. Will you tell me what's going on?
DOROTHY	The shoes are gone, the Queen can relax.
DORIS	You've set fire to all your clothes? You must have damaged your head when you fell. You've destroyed hundreds of pounds worth of clothes. Charles is going to kill you.
	(She grabs Dorothy and shakes her.)
	Are you too drunk even to realise what you've done?
DOROTHY	I'm not drunk. This is the first drink I've had since Friday night.
DORIS	Well you must have been busy on Friday night.
DOROTHY	Oh I was . . . I was.
	(Dorothy starts to laugh.)
DORIS	What are you laughing at? After what you've done . . .
DOROTHY	I'm laughing at you. If anyone came in and saw you in that hat, they'd think you were drunk.
DORIS	You're insane. You just don't seem to know what you're doing.
	(Pause)
	Look Dorothy . . . come over to my house. I'll look after you. I'll come back here and explain things to Charles. Come on.
DOROTHY	I wouldn't like to impose on Randy on a Sunday.

81

DORIS	You're just being impossible. What are you going to tell Charles?
DOROTHY	That depends . . . on whether he sees the back garden, the bathroom, or the spare room first.
	(Doris moves to go out and look. Stops.)
DORIS	Charles said you'd been drinking more recently, but I never guessed . . .
DOROTHY	I thought you said he wouldn't talk about me behind my back?
DORIS	After what you've done you needn't go looking for faults in him. If I was you I'd treat him like a Saint, and hope he gets the message and acts like one.
DOROTHY	He can count himself lucky I didn't burn this whole bloody prison down. Do you understand what I'm saying? I don't care . . . about you, about Charles, about Douglas. I don't even care about me anymore. What do I care about this bloody marriage? You don't know what you're talking about. You come in here in your church-goers', hypocrite's habit, and your funny bloody hat. Is he paying you to spy on me? Huh, if you only knew what you'd missed you could have named your price.
DORIS	I rang you on Friday night purely out of concern for you. Why didn't you ring me and tell me you were under the weather?
DOROTHY	It wasn't the weather I was under . . .
	(She is about to go on . . . stops. Drains her glass and goes for another drink. Doris gets between her and the drinks cabinet.)
DORIS	No, this has gone far enough Dorothy.
DOROTHY	Don't you dare tell me how to behave in my own house.
DORIS	You're not going to intimidate me this time. I suppose you'll set fire to me now.
DOROTHY	If you don't move aside I'll knock you out from under that hat.
DORIS	Not this time. You're getting my help whether you want it ot not.
	(She snatches Dorothy's glass.)
	There's no more drink for you today, or ever if I can help it.
DOROTHY	Just who do you think you are?
DORIS	I'm your wee sister, the Ugly Duckling. I mightn't have got many boyfriends and I can't have children. But at least I've got a happy marriage. You won't have any marriage at all, unless you let me help you.

DOROTHY	You wouldn't know where to begin, little sister. I don't need ... *(Pause)* I don't want your help.
DORIS	You said I'd always resented you, always been jealous, and you're right. I've always envied you, but I've also respected you and been proud of you. Until last week I thought you were really something. You've looks and a figure the envy of women half your age. I wouldn't be normal if I hadn't been jealous. But now you seem hell-bent on destroying yourself. I'd rather envy you your looks, than feel sorry for you because you're an alcoholic. A week ago if anyone had even suggested to me the mess you're in, I would have laughed at them. I'm angry with you because I've lost a heroine, someone I looked up to ... admired. I've always been proud to tell people you were my sister. I even enjoyed telling them you were older than me. *(Pause)*
DOROTHY	I've sharpened my wits on jibes and insults. Flattery ... compliments, I can't cope with. *(Doris removes her hat.)*
DORIS	Dad always used to say that someday we'd need each other, but we'd be too full of resentment to live it down. *(Long pause.)*
DOROTHY	Someone called here on Friday night ... just after you rang.
DORIS	But it was after eleven when I rang ... nearer half-past.
DOROTHY	I wouldn't have opened the door, but I knew him. There were two others ...
DORIS	You let three men in here at that time of night. Did you know the other two?
DOROTHY	I thought he was on his own. He got up by the way he was going to the loo, and he let the other two in.
DORIS	The nerve of some people. If it had been me I'd have put them out, all three of them, right away. How did you get rid of them?
DOROTHY	I didn't fall outside.
DORIS	Well where did you fall?
DOROTHY	I'm going to get a drink, and if you get in my way I'll tramp on you.
DORIS	Dorothy, are you saying ... *(Se gestures towards the garden, etc.)*
DOROTHY	What's the use ... there isn't an easy way to say it ... I've been raped.

83

DORIS	Christ the night girl . . . you're not serious. Tell me you're an alcoholic, or a maniac, but don't tell me that . . . You're nearly fifty.
DOROTHY	I don't think there's an upper age limit. I was raped three times, by three different men. One of them beat me . . . punched and kicked me. I don't even remember them leaving. I just remember the light coming through the window on Saturday morning. I just hurt, and bled, and cried.
	(Pause)
	About four on Saturday I struggled over here for a drink . . . I lifted his photograph and saw him grinning up at me. I could just imagine what he'd say . . . I went mad. I came back in here exhausted. I woke up on that settee at half-past two this morning.
	(Doris is crying into her hankerchief.)
DORIS	I'm going to be sick.
DOROTHY	They'll never believe me. After all his preaching . . . Charles'll be setting himself up as a fortune-teller. They did it because they fancied me . . . those good looks and lovely figure, . . . in a sexy wrapping . . . well, I've destroyed the wrappers.
DORIS	But you'll go to the police. You can't let them get away with it.
DOROTHY	They have got away with it.
DORIS	You can't tell Charles you've been raped and then refuse to go to the police.
DOROTHY	What would the police do . . . apart from sneer? They never believe you. I've suffered enough humiliation. They never believe a woman. Do you remember when Wilma Thomson took that soldier to court? Half his regiment turned up and swore they'd been to bed with her. I wasn't attacked on a dark street. I opened my own front door and I let them in.
DORIS	Opening your front door to a man doesn't give him the right to rape you.
DOROTHY	The rest of the male race gives him that right. For goodness sake, grow up. No woman can afford to lose a court case like that. Wilma went to her grave branded . . . even by me.
DORIS	But you're different, you're a respectable married woman.
DOROTHY	Anyway, these weren't just bored drunks looking for kicks. If I went to the police they'd get us . . . and if they couldn't their mates would.
	(Pause)

I'll never feel clean again.
(Pause)
Doris . . . would you hold me . . . please? Would you
just put your arms around me and hold me.
(Doris moves towards her, hesitates. They look at each
other. They embrace.)

DORIS   No woman should be left on her own in times like
                 these.
                 (Pause)

DOROTHY   Do you remember Stephen Montgomery, Douglas'
                 friend? He's the one I opened the door to.

DORIS   Stephen Montgomery?
                 (She pulls away from Dorothy.)
                 That wee lad that used to come in and out of your
                 house . . . sit at your fireside . . . eat at your table?

DOROTHY   The whole thing was his idea.
                 (Long pause.)

DORIS   I can't take that in about Stephen Montgomery. His
                 sister, Sonia, was a lovely wee girl. I'd always hoped
                 Douglas and her . . .

DOROTHY   I stopped that.

DORIS   You could have been a granny now.
                 (Pause)

DOROTHY   I want to go Doris, now . . .

DORIS   I'll explain things to Charles. If we give him a bit of
                 time I'm sure he'll understand.

DOROTHY   It doesn't matter whether he understands or not . . . I'll
                 not be coming back.

DORIS   What are you saying? Where would you go? What
                 would you do? Look, Dorothy, do or say nothing until
                 you've had time to think things over, and I've spoken
                 to Charles.

DOROTHY   I don't want you to speak to him. Christ, what are you
                 trying to do to me? This is his fault . . . that bastard.
                 He's done this to me. Do you expect me to crawl back
                 in here and live on his suffrance? Do you seriously
                 think that I can ever go back into that bedroom again?
                 Don't you understand what's happened to me?

DORIS   No, I don't understand what's happened to you. I know
                 what you've told me, but I can't begin to imagine what
                 it was like. O God, I don't even want to try. I'm only
                 asking you to wait before you make any big decisions,
                 Charles has to be given some sort of explanation. He has
                 to be told, so has Douglas. They've got to accept a
                 certain amount of responsibility for it all. You can still
                 make your own decisions in the end.

	(Pause. Doris begins to gather her things.)
	If we hang about her much longer they'll be in on top of us.
DOROTHY	What are you going to tell John when you land home with me?
DORIS	I'll tell him no more than he needs to know. Now go and get a coat.
DOROTHY	Did I leave myself a coat?
DORIS	I think I noticed a fawn raincoat in the hall. I'll get it for you.
	(She goes and fetches it, Dorothy gazes around.)
	If there's anything else you need I'll collect it later.
DOROTHY	You'll be able to carry everything over one arm. I think I left my toothbrush in one piece. I've no rollers, they're what's stuck in the loo.
DORIS	Tell me no more. Come on.
	(Doris waits at the door. She doesn't move until Dorothy starts to move. Dorothy takes a long time to gaze around, and then she moves slowly out.)

FADE.

SCENE 6

THE LIVING-ROOM. MONDAY, A FORTNIGHT LATER.

Douglas is sitting reading. Charles enters, carrying a white paper bag with half-a-dozen cassettes in it. There is a bunch of flowers, and a box of chocolates on the table.

CHARLES	Hello son.
DOUGLAS	Hello dad. What's in the bag?
CHARLES	It's just, ah, I thought maybe a few cowboy records would cheer her up.
DOUGLAS	You're trying dad.
CHARLES	Aye, I'm a bit rusty. What time are they coming?
DOUGLAS	Doris said as soon as they have their dinner she'd drop her off. She won't come in herself . . . just drop her off and then call round tomorrow.
CHARLES	Did you ask her about Wednesday night?
DOUGLAS	That's all arranged. It would have been better if it had all been over before mum got back.
CHARLES	I tried, all the men weren't available before this.
DOUGLAS	I don't think mum'll approve.
CHARLES	There's no need for her to be told.
DOUGLAS	What if it goes wrong?
CHARLES	I'd be happier if you'd stay here with your mother. We can manage without you.
DOUGLAS	You just let me have Montgomery, and stop me just before I kill him.
CHARLES	This isn't going to be a bloody picnic you know. Take it serious.
DOUBLAS	I'm taking it serious, believe me.
CHARLES	Those bastards aren't going to give us any second chance, Have you seen Montgomery around?
DOUGLAS	He's around all right. I just look at him and think about which of his bones I'm going to break.
CHARLES	Be careful, don't give him the slightest hint. I want those three bastards together, just the way . . .
DOUGLAS	What are we going to use?
CHARLES	Don't worry, we'll have any God's amount of stuff from the site.
DOUGLAS	But no guns?

87

CHARLES	We'll have what's necessary.
	(Pause)
	Did you have something to eat?
DOUGLAS	I'd a snack before I came in. I'd a big feed at lunchtime. What about you?
CHARLES	Christ, I can't eat.
DOUGLAS	How must she be feeling?
CHARLES	Maybe we're all expecting too much of each other. That's what worries me. There are some things I can't imagine ever being the same again.
DOUGLAS	As Aunt Doris says, you've got to forgive her now because you want to. Not later on because you're beginning to forget.
CHARLES	You wouldn't half know she went to church.
	(Pause)
	The night your mother phoned . . . we just breathed at each other for ten minutes. She didn't sound like she wanted me to forgive her when she did start . . . She made it sound the other way round. She sounds like she's going to use that spare-room like a flat.
	(Pause)
	Do you think them perfumes and stuff's all right?
DOUGLAS	Great. Mind you, I've never known mum to have pimples.
CHARLES	Pimples! Your mother never had a pimple in her life.
DOUGLAS	That's what I'm saying. Two of those tubes you bought clear up acne and blackheads . . . fast.
CHARLES	Ah . . . Jasus.
DOUGLAS	It's all right, I've taken them out. I put them in the medicine cupboard, along with the stuff for the haemorrhoids.
CHARLES	Haemorrhoids! For crying out bloody loud . . .
DOUGLAS	Relax dad, I'm joking.
CHARLES	This is no time for bloody jokes.
	(Pause)
	Do you think I should have bought her a new dress?
DOUGLAS	Don't get too ambitious. She wouldn't trust you to buy her shroud.
CHARLES	What the hell's keeping them? Do you think it's wise to offer her a drink?
DOUGLAS	I think it's essential.
CHARLES	Does she take it neat?
DOUGLAS	For goodness sake dad, how long have you been married?
CHARLES	Long enough to have forgotten details like that.

(Charles fixes a drink. Checks around. Touches-up flowers, repositions chocolates.)

88

DOUGLAS	Should we put on one of her cowboy records as she comes in?
CHARLES	I might have bought those records, but I draw the line at having to listen to them. They're either laying flowers on somebody's grave, or taking their broken hearts on a pub-crawl.
	(He sits.)
	Sssssshh . . . was that a car?
	(He jumps up.)
	It was, Jasus, she's here . . . open the door . . . let her in. It's lemonade isn't it. Gin and lemonade . . .
	(Douglas goes to the door.)
DOUGLAS	Will you calm down dad, otherwise she'll spend the next fortnight watching you strapped to a heart machine.
	(Dorothy enters, Douglas behind her. She is wearing a "sober" woollen suit. Charles stands, a glass with gin in one hand, lemonade in the other.)
CHARLES	I've a drink here . . . there's flowers, some chocolates. Is it white lemonade you take in your drink?
DOROTHY	I'll just have the white lemonade.
CHARLES	In gin?
DOROTHY	White lemonade, in a glass.
	(He brings her a white lemonade.)
	The place is looking very . . . clean.
CHARLES	We spent the whole weekend on it. We thought you'd like it.
DOROTHY	You did it for me? I thought you did it because you live here too.
CHARLES	How's John?
DOROTHY	He's fine.
CHARLES	Randy?
DOROTHY	Fine, he sleeps most of the time . . . in his new bed.
CHARLES	That's a nice suit.
DOROTHY	It's new. I'll have to put it on a hanger tonight.
CHARLES	Well, at least there'll be plenty of room for it . . . it'll ah, not be crushed.
	(Pause)
	Do you like the flowers?
DOROTHY	They're lovely. They brighten the place up.
CHARLES	Some ah, . . . I thought maybe . . . a few cowboy records.
DOROTHY	Lovely . . . thank you.
CHARLES	Doris left you at the door then?
DOUGLAS	For goodness sake . . . mum, dad, look . . . we don't have to talk. We can just sit here . . .
	(Pause)
DOROTHY	We do have to talk. I can't just slip back here, after a

	fortnight, after all that's happened. We can't just carry on as if nothing had happened, as if nothing had changed.
DOUGLAS	But tonight . . . do we have to start tonight?
DOROTHY	The sooner we talk about it the better.
	(Pause)
DOUGLAS	Maybe we should have prepared notes. Will I ask questions?
CHARLES	Douglas! Doris has been very good Dorothy. She's given us time . . .
DOROTHY	Do you believe me Charles?
CHARLES	Of course I believe you.
DOROTHY	Do you believe all of it?
DOUGLAS	Mum, we're all back together again aren't we?
DOROTHY	Do you believe it happened the way I said?
	(Pause)
	You don't, do you Charles?
CHARLES	I believe what happened to you.
DOROTHY	You bastard . . . Christ I might have known. Why don't you just come out and say, "I told you so." Why don't you have the guts to say what you're thinking? Flowers, and chocolates, and cowboy records. You make me sick.
DOUGLAS	We shouldn't be talking about these things tonight. We're not . . .
DOROTHY	Shut you up spluttering.
	(To Charles.)
	You think I was messing about, don't you?
DOUGLAS	No he does not.
DOROTHY	I'm waiting for him to say it.
DOUGLAS	Come on dad, tell her that's not what you think.
DOROTHY	Of course it's what he thinks, look at his face.
DOUGLAS	Dad, will you say something?
CHARLES	Why did you open the door?
	(She rises.)
DOROTHY	I'm going.
CHARLES	Why don't you just answer me?
DOROTHY	I opened the door because it was Stephen. I knew him . . . He was a friend of Douglas' . . . He was a friend of the family . . . I didn't think anything, I just opened the door.
CHARLES	Were the others at the door?
DOROTHY	Yes, they were, and a dozen others representing a broad cross-section of the population. They all carried a different coloured durex and asked me if I'd help them make a rainbow.
CHARLES	I only asked you a civil question.
DOROTHY	A civil question! "Excuse me darling, did you

	consent to the rape or was it forced on you?" What kind of a civil question's that? If you'd been here, if you'd cared about me, it wouldn't have happened.
CHARLES	If I'd been here. Jasus Christ woman, I need some life of my own.
DOUGLAS	Shut up! Listen mum. I believe you. I believe every single word you said. I told him, when he was ranting and raving about it, that if he wanted to get mad at anybody, then he should get mad at the ones who did it to you. We know who they are and we're going to get the bastards.
DOROTHY	Get them . . . how? What do you mean?
DOUGLAS	Dad got some of his workmen to find out who they are. It's all fixed up for Wednesday night. *(Pause. She looks at Charles.)*
CHARLES	Doris give us names. I got men to find out about them. We're going to get them.
DOROTHY	But you can't. They'll kill you. They're not just journeymen rapists, they're in one of the organisations.
CHARLES	I know that, but you're forgetting my "common" background. I know the score. I've had to handle characters like that all my life. They don't frighten me.
DOROTHY	They've killed bigger men than you.
CHARLES	Look, raping you wasn't an official job. Nobody's going to lift a hand to help them.
DOROTHY	I'll go to the police. If we're going to take risks let's at least do it the sensible way.
CHARLES	We are, we're doing it the only way it'll work for us. People lie down and let these characters walk all over them. Nobody's ever called their bluff.
DOROTHY	Why don't you check that in your local cemetery. If you care about me at all . . . stay here . . . for me.
CHARLES	We're doing this for all of us. They're going to get the hiding of their lives. They'll not rape anyone anymore when we're finished with them.
DOROTHY	How did you get the others to agree to go with you?
CHARLES	Money.
DOROTHY	Money! Christ, a sponsored suicide. And you trust them? Do you seriously think they'll risk their lives for money? Do I just sit here and wait for the police to tell me where to pick up your bodies?
CHARLES	You'll not be on your own. Doris is coming round to sit with you.
DOROTHY	Good God. The team that brought you reconciliation, now brings you total devastation.

91

CHARLES   Even if you hadn't come back I'd have had to do this.
           Do you remember when we bought this site? It was a
           journey we made together. Those three bastards have
           dragged you back down the hill, and you had to come
           up it again on your own. I have to do the same. I
           have to go back down there . . . and come up again.
           We can't go anywhere until I've done that. It doesn't
           matter about them and whether they're bluffing or
           not, this is about us.
DOROTHY   Those fellas don't stop at the sight of blood, they only
           really start then.
           (Long pause.)
           What are you leaving me with, if they're not bluffing?
           (Pause)
CHARLES   At least you'll know what I was, and how much I really
           thought of you.
           (Pause)

           FADE

92

SCENE 7

LIVING ROOM. WEDNESDAY NIGHT.

Doris is sitting knitting.

DOROTHY	It's nearly midnight. What on earth's keeping them?
DORIS	They said it would probably be well after midnight.
DOROTHY	This is taking years out of me. By the time he gets back I'll be too old for him. I should never have let them go. I'm surprised that you approved of it. You even encouraged them.
DORIS	In the end you can only live with the truth.
DOROTHY	Honestly Doris, talking to you is like having a conversation with the New English Bible. *(Pause)* Do you remember my baby?
DORIS	Wee Dorothy . . . of course I remember her.
DOROTHY	Dorothy wasn't her name. She didn't have a name, we hadn't decided. I called her Dorothy because I wanted to die with her. I know you won't believe me now . . . but I was going to call her after you, Sarah Doris Williams.
DORIS	Why didn't you tell me?
DOROTHY	She would have got Sarah, but your name would have been there. You'd just missed again and I felt sorry for you. I also felt guilty about the way I'd treated you. It was Charles, he didn't agree. He didn't like Sarah. He said it wasn't fair to call her after my mother and my sister. Douglas was called after dad. He wanted her called after his mother . . . Masie. Do you know what I said? *(Pause)* I said she'd be better off dead than to have a name like that. I've always been too quick with my tongue. When she died I knew how you felt, but I hated you because I knew you knew how I felt.
DORIS	You screamed at me on the day of the funeral. You accused me of gloating. You said I'd never brought anything but dead meat into the world. I swore I'd never speak to you again. I think it's still been between us all these years.

93

DOROTHY	I hated everybody that day, every day for weeks . . . especially Charles. I didn't speak a word to him for weeks.
	(Pause)
	There's only been one night in my life when I was glad she wasn't here. She'd have been seventeen now. Imagine a daughter of that age. She'd have been great company. We could have gone out every Saturday, for make-up, and clothes . . .
	(Pause)
	I just wanted you to know.
DORIS	Thanks.
DOROTHY	What time did you tell John you'd be home?
DORIS	I told him to expect me when he sees me, or rather when he feels me. He'll be in bed when I get back.
DOROTHY	I thought you never talked about things like that?
DORIS	Here now, just because you've got a remoulded marriage. I meant he'd feel my cold feet.
DOROTHY	Feet can be romantic, if they're well placed. He's talking about buying a new double bed.
DORIS	Huh, it's as well this didn't happen a few years ago or you'd be expecting another . . .
	(Pause)
DOROTHY	Another wee Sarah Doris.
DORIS	I'm sorry, it just slipped out.
DOROTHY	It's all right.
	(Pause)
	We waited too long afterwards. It was my fault as much as his . . . but I blamed him.
DORIS	I did envy you when I saw her . . . I would have loved her too.
DOROTHY	I wish I could have one now.
DORIS	Why don't you adopt one?
DOROTHY	Come on now Doris, let's have one problem you don't have an instant solution for. If I took your advice the house would be full of babies, and dogs, and I'd be out working.
	(Pause)
	Actually I've been thinking I might try and do some of Charles' office work here at home. I could buy a typewriter.
DORIS	I used to help John to do his books, but with my counting we were always falling out.
DOROTHY	Oh . . . I thought you two didn't?
DORIS	Well that was different. That was more disagreements about figures. Anyway, I think it's a great idea for

94

DOROTHY	you. In fact, why don't you work in the office on the site and get out of the house for a while?
DOROTHY	His name's Williams, not Wimpy. The office is just a wee wooden hut, with attached port-a-loo. I can't quite see myself in that kind of set-up. Mind you it might be nice to have our rows on location. *(Pause)* I wish to God they'd hurry up.
DORIS	I'm sure . . . what was that?
DOROTHY	What? I didn't hear anything.
DORIS	I thought I heard a noise like glass breaking somewhere.
DOROTHY	You're imagining things. Maybe someone down the avenue's dropped a milk bottle. *(Pause)* What's going on down there? What are they doing? Surely to God . . .
DORIS	Look Dorothy, when this is over we'll have to get together. You'll have to visit us, and we'll visit you. Properly, with Charles and John, the way it should be. Maybe you and I could go down the town an odd Saturday, the way other sisters do. What do you say? *(Pause)*
DOROTHY	Just let me get through tonight Doris and you, and John, and Randy, can come and live with us if you like.
DORIS	Do you know girl I feel an awful draught, have you left a door or a window open somewhere?
DOROTHY	I've maybe left a window open in the kitchen. I'll just check. *(Just as she rises the doorbell rings.)* They're back . . . thank goodness. I told Charles not to forget his key, that man!
DORIS	I'll go and check that window and put the kettle on. *(They exit accordingly. After a few seconds Dorothy returns.)*
DOROTHY	There's nobody there. I checked through the spyhole. I couldn't see . . . *(Pause)* Doris! Doris . . . are you there? *(She goes towards the kitchen. The door opens, she freezes, Andy appears. He carries a knapsack.)*
ANDY	You'd better open that front door missus. You know Mike doesn't like to be kept waiting. *(Pause. He moves towards her as the doorbell rings again.)* Go and open that door missus . . . and hurry up about it.

	(She does so and returns with Mike, him leading.)
DOROTHY	Where's Doris?
MIKE	Never heard tell of her.
DOROTHY	She was here with me she's my sister . . .
ANDY	She's just having a wee lie down.
DOROTHY	Where's Charles and Douglas?
MIKE	The lady thinks we've opened a missing persons agency.
DOROTHY	I want to see Doris.
MIKE	Go and fetch her sister Andy. I'd like to have a squint at her too.

(Andy goes.)
This is just like coming home Dorothy.
(Andy comes back, pushing Doris before him. She has a bruise on her cheek and her glasses are missing. She sits, Dorothy comes and stands behind her.)

DORIS	My glasses Dorothy.
MIKE	Go and get Dorothy's big sister her glasses Andy.

(Andy goes.)
Isn't this dead romantic, a foursome.
(Andy returns with the glasses on the end of his nose. Mike holds out his hand.)
I'm very pleased to meet you Doris. Any sister of Dorothy's and all that. I'm Mike. Andy believes in making an immediate impact.

DOROTHY	Mike, where's Charles?
MIKE	Between my legs . . . don't be impatient. Your sister's a bull for it Doris. Do you perform?
DORIS	I'm a housewife.
MIKE	Do you ride?
DORIS	I did, once or twice years ago, but I don't anymore.
MIKE	Why not?
DORIS	I don't have a horse.
MIKE	Doesn't every family have one like that eh? My young brother Matt, fella asked him one day if he was a virgin. He said he never discussed religion.
DOROTHY	Please Mike what have you done with them?
MIKE	I haven't seen them. I knew they were coming to see me tonight. One of the men Charlie Boy tried to hire happens to be a great mate of mine. Told me a very interesting story. I've just decided to change a few things. I thought it would be much nicer if we all met back here. Go and get the stuff Andy. We'll need two chairs, and some more cord. See about two more bits of cloth.

(Andy goes.)
We didn't expect two for the price of one . . . cheap

96

women. Never mind, I'll not show any favouritism.
(Andy returns with two dining-room chairs, strong cord and cloth. He places the two chairs. Takes more material from his bag.)
Let me just explain Ladies. I'm sure you'll agree no party's complete without games. After we've tied you to these chairs we're going to sneak away and hide. When Charlie and Dougie return we'll all play a nice game of hide and seek.

DORIS   My husband's calling for me. He'll be here any minute.

MIKE   Great, the more the merrier.

DORIS   He's a policeman.

MIKE   And where would we be without them? My old granda used to say that no game of hide and seek was complete without a policeman. Now . . . sit in your chairs.
(Dorothy nods to Doris and they do so.)
Obedience is a beautiful game to watch.
(Andy starts tying Doris.)
It's great having the two of you tonight. Two of you, two of us . . . and the other two. We're going to have great fun. You ladies'll just amaze yourselves, the things you'll be prepared to do for us.

DOROTHY   Is Charles safe?

MIKE   Lady you are just obsessed. He's fine and just raring to repeat his last performance.

DOROTHY   For crying out loud Mike, just tell me what's happened to him, please.

MIKE   He's a nasty man that. I don't know what a nice lady like you ever saw in him, unless he's well called. What do you say Andy?

ANDY   That man's a walking bastard missus. Got a big gang up for us.

DOROTHY   Then you saw him?

MIKE   From a distance. I couldn't deny myself the pleasure of watching them take Stephen. We kept all this a surprise from Stephen. He's been complaining about toothache all week and I thought, well, two birds with one stone. Your precious Douglas hit him. A pick-axe handle right across the mouth. It was a really beautiful stroke. We weren't close enough to hear the teeth breaking, but you could just imagine it . . . a beautiful crinkling sound. Then the blood spurted out. Just what Belfast needs on a dull Wednesday night . . . a nice splash of colour. I've bet Andy a pound that he'll not make as nice a mess of Douglas' mouth.

97

	(Andy has just completed blindfolding and gagging Doris.)
	Thank goodness you've managed to shut that woman up at last.
DOROTHY	We'll give you a thousand pounds.
MIKE	Oh I know, and lots of other wee things as well.
DOROTHY	Mike I begged him not to do it. I told him you were too tough for him, too clever. He wouldn't listen. He's only doing it for me. You're a man, surely you can understand that?
MIKE	Of course, I respect him Dorothy.
DOROTHY	And Douglas, he's young and headstrong. I'm his mother. He's doing it for me. I know you love your mother . . . wouldn't you do the same for her?
	(Mike's stomach is beginning to trouble him.)
MIKE	You think I'm an idiot don't you?
DOROTHY	No I don't, honestly. You wouldn't be here if you were an idot. Dont hurt them Mike, I'll do anything you say . . . absolutely anything . . . but please don't hurt them.
ANDY	Do you think we're doing all this for nothing missus? We have to have some fun.
MIKE	Is her husband a policeman?
DOROTHY	She didn't know Mike, she was afraid . . .
	(He starts pulling at Doris's hair.)
MIKE	That's the sort of lying that can upset my stomach. They kept me in hospital four days the last time. I've stopped drinking . . . but all this excitement and all tonight . . . it could get bad.
	(He punches Doris in the stomach.)
	I could get really nasty if it gets bad.
DOROTHY	Don't hurt her Mike. She's only here to keep me company.
MIKE	Do you know something Dorothy, everybody's doing everything for you, eh? Even us, it's because of you we're here too. We'll all have to wear badges, "I did it for Dorothy". But I've still got some things to do for Dorothy.
	(The phone rings. Mike visibly jumps. He looks nervously from Dorothy to Andy. He checks his watch. It rings six or seven times and then stops.)
ANDY	Who the fuck was that?
MIKE	Were you expecting a call? Who do you think that was?
DOROTHY	Probably my bank manager to tell me my shares have dipped.
MIKE	Now listen you . . .

98

DOROTHY	I know . . . that's the sort of thing that could start your stomach. Don't worry, there's enough milk for you to have a bath in. You're finished Mike.
MIKE	Finished! I'm finished? You're sitting there tied to your chairs, completely at my mercy . . . one word from me and you're dead. Your dear Charles, and your dear Douglas are about to walk into my trap . . .
DOROTHY	Are they?
MIKE	You're mixing up your starters and finishers Dorothy.
ANDY	I'll cut her fucking throat.
MIKE	Andy!
DOROTHY	Leave him alone Mike. Come on Andy, cut my fucking throat. Show Mike how good you really were, because it doesn't matter anymore.
	(Pause)
	(Andy and Mike look at each other. Mike glances at the telephone.)
	All right, you can beat us up, rape us, kill us. You can do whatever you like to us, but you're finished. Even if you just walked out through that door and left us now, you're in trouble. The longer you stay here, and the more you do to us, the worse it's going to be for you. We're from down there.
	(Mike and Andy glance at each other, surprised.)
	You didn't even know that much, did you?
MIKE	You know nothing about down there, nothing. You don't know about the bombs and the murders, and the shit we have to live in because of people like you. Oh aye, you can look across the Lough and see green fields. You don't even have to look down. You don't have to know about the shit and the people who live in it, people like us.
	(Mike's pains are increasing.)
	After tonight we're going to make sure you remember us. We'll show Charlie Boy that we count.
DOROTHY	Charles was born down there, they know him. He's got friends down there, friends who are bigger than you. They'll see you pay for this.
MIKE	Who?
DOROTHY	I was wrong about you Mike. You are a fool. You're an even bigger fool than . . .
	(Pause)
	(Dorothy is completely tied now, except for her gag.)
	You're all fools . . .
	(Andy puts her gag on. He then goes and starts rummaging in his bag. He takes out two revolvers and places them on

99

	the floor. Then he goes into the bedroom with the bag.
	Mike goes across and takes out a bottle of whiskey. He
	moves over to the stereo unit. He is swigging from the
	bottle.)
MIKE	Old Charlie Boy must really love you, eh? I can

Old Charlie Boy must really love you, eh? I can understand that. I can even understand him getting mad, especially after what Andy did to you, but that was a sort of an accident. Even so Dorothy there are things he's got to realise. We're not going to let people like you go on running our lives. We'll give you a few wee problems tonight that'll keep you occupied, keep you out of our business.

(He checks his watch.)

It's time. Charles has got a message . . . he should be on his way home by now.

(Pause)

Do you know what I'll be thinking about until he arrives Dorothy? I'll be thinking about what I'd be suffering now . . .

(He is almost doubled in pain.)

. . . if my friend hadn't tipped me off.

(Andy comes back in. The empty knapsack crumpled in his hand. When he sees the state Mike is in he stops. He looks around slowly, drops the knapsack and picks up the two revolvers. He is going to offer one to Mike. Mike puts the cassette on. Don Williams sings, "Gipsy Woman". Andy puts one of the guns in his pocket.)

F A D E

THE END

THE HIDDEN CURRICULUM

For Joanna Marston

CAST

TONY CAIRNS	Head of English Department
DAVID DUNN	Teacher, English & History
WINIFRED WALKER (Miss)	In charge of remedial work
FRANK MERCER	Head of History Department
HERBERT MONTGOMERY	Headmaster
TOM ALLEN	Ex-pupil
BILL BOYD	Ex-pupil
ERIC ALEXANDER	Father of ex-pupil
RUBY	Eric's woman
BRICKSO	Local tough
ARCHIE	Local tough
MAUREEN BAXTER	Pupil
ANN WILSON	Pupil

The play is set in West Belfast, mid to late seventies.

ACT ONE

SCENE 1

Allen and Boyd on the street. Ann Wilson passes on her way to school.

BOYD   Hey sexy, got your knickers in your schoolbag? *(Whistling)*

ANN   *(Stopping and looking him up and down).* Have you lost your dog?

ALLEN: If he'd lost his dog he wouldn't be whistling at a bitch like you.

ANN   Very funny ... if you two'd go and get a job it would answer yous better. *(Stomps off).*

BOYD   Checky wee shite.

ALLEN   She's a quare pair of sticks on her though ... a quare oul body for a schoolgirl.

SCENE 2

(Open — Allen and Boyd on the street. Tony Cairns, book in hand, reading to his class. A loud siren builds ... passes and then fades.)

TONY   *(Sharply)* All right, Thompson, sit down. You have seen an ambulance before today, it doesn't concern us. *(Pause)* Thompson! If I have to speak to you again boy, you'll be in after school today. Now pay attention. *(He scans the book again ... Reads with great attention, absorbed by the details)* "... drags off with a great wound in his back through which the lung pulses at every breath. I can only press his hand. 'It's all up, Paul', he groans and he bites his arm because of the pain.

"We see men living with their skulls blown open; we see soldiers run with their two feet cut off, they stagger on their splintered limbs into the next shell-hole; a lance-corporal crawls a mile and a half on his hands

102

dragging his smashed knee after him; another goes to the dressing station and over his clasped hands bulge his intestines; we see men without mouths, without jaws, without faces; we find one man who has held the artery of his arm in his teeth for two hours in order not to bleed to death. The sun goes down, night comes, the shells whine, life is at an end.
"Still the little piece of convulsed earth in which we lie is held. We have yielded no more than a few hundred yards of it as a prize to the enemy. But on every yard their lies a dead man." *(Pause)* Now ... take a note of your homework for Monday. Write a detailed critical appreciation of Owens' poem, "Dulce Et Decorum Est". It is on page seventy-three of your poetry books, and I want to see a considerable improvement on last time. *(Pause)* Beattie ... I'll be paying particular attention to your effort, you appear to find all of this highly amusing. It's not amusing, not in the least. A lot of Ulstermen died in the Great War. Thousands of Protestants, UVF men and Orangemen. Many of them went over the top wearing their sashes, singing orange songs or shouting "No Surrender". Some of your grandfathers and great-grandfathers were probably amongst them. They lived in those streets down there, in those same little houses you live in. This is about *your* history, *your* backgrounds. *(Pause)* Does it not strike you as odd that I should know more about your backgrounds than you do? Some of you are in the Orange Order, I'm not. Does it not strike you as odd, Thompson ... Beattie ... and the rest of you sniggerers, that I should care more about your backgrounds than you do? *(Pause)* It is high time you all became a lot more aware of the world around you. It's time you cared about what is going on. *(Pause. The bell sounds for the end of the period)* Sit still ... who told you to pack up? Creighton, take that scarf off. We're all feeling the cold but there's no need to exaggerate boy. *(Pause)* Put your books away. Now we'll file out quietly, one row at a time. *(Pause)* Right. *(Fade)*

SCENE 3

(The street. Allen and Boyd standing. Boyd is gazing up the street, to stage right.)

BOYD Look at them all rushing to school.

ALLEN At least they've somewhere to go.

BOYD Look at Fat Joe's coat. Wouldn't you think his ma would buy him a new one?

ALLEN Sure he's leaving this year, there's no point.

BOYD Aye, but it's been like that for about three years. *(Shouting)* Hey, Joe ... Fat Man ... hey, did you get that coat from Oxenfam? *(Laughs but stops and expression changes at Fat Joe obviously makes some visual response)* Cheeky bastard ... you know some day I'll rattle his nuts for him, fat bollocks.

ALLEN *(Laughs at Boyd's expense)* Y'know, I reckon Fat Joe could take you.

BOYD What? I know . . . I'd bate him and his brother.

ALLEN I don't know, he's a strong wee bugger.

BOYD Strong's nothing, the oul nut and a kick on the stones and Fat Man's finished.

ALLEN He give Big Skinso a good go.

BOYD Aye, but Skinso was pissed. *(Pause. Rubs his hands and stamps his feet)* It would skin the monks of a brass ballsy. Hey, that's a good one, isn't it?

ALLEN Great . . . Do you ever miss school?

BOYD Aye . . . but only when I'm too far away and the stone's heavy.

ALLEN *(Gazing off stage left)* I'm bored already. Here come the lads.
(Brickso and Archie amble on. Muttered greetings and nods)

BOYD Where you for, lads?

ARCHIE Big Smicks and Ben are in court this morning for stealing drink. Are you coming down?

ALLEN Naw, couldn't be bothered.

BRICKSO Well, listen, don't just be standing there doing nothing ... Eric booked an early call.
(They laugh and exit stage right. Light comes up on Alexander's living room. The door is kicked and banged loudly)

BOYD You still in there, Alexander? *(Eric enters partially dressed. He wears trousers and a shirt not yet buttoned. He has one shoe on and carries the other and a jumper)* Come on, Alexander, it's time to go time and take your whore with you.

RUBY	*(Entering in dressing gown)* Who is it?
ERIC	*(Glaring at her)* It's the Salvation Army carol singers.
RUBY	I only asked.
ERIC	Who the hell do you think it is? *(Opens the hall door, careful not to stand directly in front of the outside door)* You're brave on the other side of a locked door. Why don't you have the guts to face me?
ALLEN	You're running out of time, Alexander and we're running out of patience.
ERIC	You'll not force me out . . . this is my house. I was born here and I'll die here.
BOYD	*(Laughing)* Any day now, unless you go . . . and your whore.
	(More loud banging on the door . . . and then silence)
ERIC	Bastards. Rotten, gutless bastards. *(Pause)*
RUBY	We can't go on like this, Eric. It isn't worth it. We're prisoners, rats in a trap. *(Pacing about, distracted)* You said they'd stop. You said they weren't serious? You said it was only a few young ones who'd get tired of it. You said . . .
ERIC	All right . . . Jasus woman, is what they're doing not bad enough without you drivin' me nuts?
RUBY	What about me . . . ? I think I must be nuts already . . . otherwise I'd have left the night they broke the windows.
ERIC	I'm not forcing you to stay.
RUBY	Eric, I lay awake last night . . . all night. We can't . . . I can't go on. I can't . . . not any longer. It was ten past three this morning when they started smashing those bottles against the boards on the windows. I thought it was petrol bombs . . . and some of these nights it will be. *(Pause)* I'll go with you anywhere . . . but if you won't go, I'll have to.
ERIC	From the first day you moved in here, you've been threatening to move out for one reason or another. If you're going, go don't forget to close the door behind you. *(He turns to go)*
RUBY	I'm serious you know, I've had enough.
ERIC	Five past nine . . . schoolboys. Bloody schoolboys'll never drive me out.
RUBY	They weren't schoolboys at three o'clock this morning.
ERIC	Drunks . . . throwing away their empty bottles.
RUBY	Isn't it drunks who do everything in this place?
ERIC	Aye, well you'd know all about that.
RUBY	I'll give you until the end of the week . . .
ERIC	Again . . . you haven't missed a week for months.

105

RUBY	What are you stayin here for, a brick slum? Look at it ... look at us ... boards over all the windows ... darkness all the time. We're like insects living in a cave. What are we doing it for?
ERIC	My da wrought all his days to buy this place ... scrimped and saved, so that he'd have this to pass on to me. This was the only bought house in the street. That's what my da did for me ... his son.
RUBY	Well, if you're waiting to do the same, forget it. You'll be dead before they ever let him out.
ERIC	Roy'll be out ... and I'll be here waiting.
RUBY	You're forgetting ...
ERIC	Shut up.
RUBY	He got life ... and life ... and life ... and life.
ERIC	I'm warning you ... you leave Roy out of it, he's my son.
RUBY	Your son ... you were there, you heard what the Judge said ... life should mean life ... and who put him there? Who got us into this mess?
ERIC	He put himself there. I did him a favour.
RUBY	Tell them that when they come kicking the door. You got him involved in the first place, Commander Alexander. Then you go and get him put away for good, forever. Now tell me who you're keeping this bloody pig-sty for? *(This attack shatters Eric and Ruby immediately regrets it. Pause)*
ERIC	They're going to destroy us ... one way or another.
RUBY	I'm sorry, Eric ...
ERIC	If you want to go, go ... I'm staying.
RUBY	I haven't stayed all this time because I love the house. *(Pause)*
ERIC	*(Going)* Call me when the breakfast's ready.
RUBY	There's nothing for the bloody breakfast.
ERIC	There's a couple of shillings in my coat, go and buy some eggs.
RUBY	You go ... by the time I get dressed and ready ...
ERIC	You don't need all dressed up. You're going to buy eggs, not serve in a lounge bar.
RUBY	Sure if you go I'll have the tea and toast ready for you coming back. *(He buttons his shirt, puts on his jumper and shoe. Ties his shoes.)*
ERIC	I was born in this house, this street. I know them all. I know their das, aye and their das' das too.

106

RUBY	You broke the rules . . . wouldn't you have condemned someone else?
ERIC	He was my son, my only son and I put the finger on him . . . do they think that was easy for me? You think I was wrong?
RUBY	No, no . . . I think you were half-right . . . getting away from here's the other half of it.
	(Allen and Boyd return to the street)
ERIC	Why don't you leave me?
RUBY	Why? I suppose I hope it's going to be as good as we said at the beginning. Why did you have Roy put away? Why do you stay here? Why don't we just set fire to each other?
	(He rises ready to go. Slow fade on house. Lights up on street)
BOYD	*(Mimicing Eric)* Why don't you have the guts to face me?
	(They laugh)
ALLEN	Hey, he's coming . . . *(As Boyd makes to run)* No . . . stay here. *(Pause)*
	(Eric enters from stage right. He stops beside Allen and Boyd)
ERIC	Did you see anybody at my door a while ago?
BOYD	What, you mean the postman like?
ALLEN	We're not long here, Mr Alexander, didn't see anybody.
ERIC	If I get my hands on the gets who kicked that door, I'll bloody strangle them.
BOYD	It's probably some of the wee fellas going to school. They're always raking about.
ERIC	It's no kids. I don't suppose it was you two?
ALLEN	Us? We've only got here.
ERIC	Oh no . . . nobody round here ever does anything. You'll do it once too often.
BOYD	What are you mouthing about, it wasn't us.
ERIC	*(Pointing)* I'll take none of your lip.
BOYD	It wasn't us.
ERIC	I'm the man would put you on your back soon enough, sonny.
BOYD	*(Cowed)* We didn't do nothin'.
ALLEN	We're just standing here, Mr Alexander. We haven't seen anybody.
	(Eric looks at them in disgust, then walks away. Boyd does the two finger sign to his back)
BOYD	We should have kicked the door in.
ALLEN	Maybe he will think it was the ones from the school

	and go up to oul Monty and complain. Do you remember Monty's wee stories in the Assembly? *(Mimics)* Now some bad boys and girls, and we know they aren't pupils at our school ... 'Member the day we were all trying to piss over the toilet wall and he give you a big boot up the arse?
BOYD	I suppose they're all still up there, Monty, Talbot, Dunn and oul Ma Walker. She used to make us all say, "A boy who can't read will always be in need", 'member?
ALLEN	I could read, I didn't have to go to her.
BOYD	Oul Frank the Wank.
ALLEN	Mercer . . . he used to bore me.
BOYD	He used to always fart. 'Member the day he farted when he was showing the war film. Hillso said he could smell the gas ... Mercer slapped his lugs.
ALLEN	Remember Cairnsy?
BOYD	Moany Tony . . . he used to cry when he read oul poems.
ALLEN	He used to always tell me I was good.
BOYD	He used to say I was good . . . for nothin'.
ALLEN	Hey, do you fancy going up to see them?
BOYD	What, back up there, are you wise?
ALLEN	Come on, it'll be a rake.
BOYD	I'm not going up there, I hated that place.
ALLEN	Aye, but it was different then . . . they can't push us around now.
BOYD	I'd like to see them try it . . . oul Dunn tries any pushing or shoving I'll drop him. Hey, do you remember the day Hillso stole Ma Walker's glasses?
ALLEN	I told you I didn't do special reading.
BOYD	He put them down on her chair and she set on them. Ripped the arse of herself. *(They roar with laughter)*
ALLEN	Come on, it'll be a laugh.
BOYD	Naw, not on a Friday, maybe some other day. *(Eric returns with his eggs)*
ERIC	You two, clear off.

(Allen and Boyd exit, laughing, Eric opens door)
(Fade lights for scene change)

SCENE 4

(A small staffroom. There is a boiler for making tea,
etc. Easy chairs, tables. The latter cluttered with books.
Winifred enters with Frank. She is in her late fifties, she
carries a basket. He is sixty-two. He carries a large
flask and a lunchbox.)

FRANK   I tell you if I was headmaster I'd drill a hole in the
damned oil tank and close for a week.

WINIFRED   Oh Frank, you wouldn't.

FRANK   Who is he trying to impress? Half the schools in the
country are closed or closing. Someone should tell him
this is a ramshackle Belfast secondary school, not the
Windmill bloody Theatre. *(Pause)* How come we've so
much bloody oil anyway?

WINIFRED   Dunn says our Headmaster's new mistress is an Arab
princess.

FRANK   Must be something. I'd love a few days off. It's too
damned cold to be conscientious. When are we going
to have another oil strike?

WINIFRED   Well, if it goes off early today I'm going to complain.

FRANK   Why wait, it goes off at two o'clock every day. The
time-switch is set.

WINIFRED   A friend rang me last night. They had a staff meeting
in their school on Friday and were told not to come in
this week at all, unless the strike is called off before
Wednesday.

FRANK   I keep pointedly explaining the situation to my fourth
formers. We have the most efficient vandals in Belfast,
and they still can't take a hint.

WINIFRED   Really, Frank . . . Dunn says he'll do it himself if the
boys don't.

FRANK   Dunn! He'll attack it with his head and only succeed
in knocking himself out.

WINIFRED   He's quite capable of doing it though.

FRANK   If Dunn could find a way of marrying theory to
practice, he'd rule the world. *(Pours himself some tea)*

WINIFRED   Maybe there'll be a poor attendance, seeing so many
others are closed.

FRANK   Huh, nothing ever makes that much difference. I'm
sure if we had been teaching during the Plague we
would have had full classes. We thought we would
have lost a few during internment. The only person we
eventually lost was the bloody caretaker.

WINIFRED   Sure three years and this will all be over for you.

FRANK   Huh, three years and everything will be over for me.

109

WINIFRED   Nonsense, you're as strong as a horse.
FRANK   The strongest horse is only a leg-break away from the
           knackers yard. *(He starts working at a pile of books. It
           should be obvious that he's just giving the work a very
           cursory glance and merely marking the page)* Do you
           know, sometimes I have nightmares about marking
           books?
WINIFRED   It doesn't do to let a job dominate one's life. I'm sure
           shipyard workers don't worry about their work the
           way we do.
FRANK   I spent most of the weekend marking first-form history
           papers.
WINIFRED   Well, there you are now. It's unhealthy ... you should
           forget about work altogether from three-thirty on
           Friday, until nine-fifteen on Monday.
FRANK   Those history papers. Do you know, one little madam
           said the English called William the Conqueror a
           bastard because he beat them.
WINIFRED   She used that word, in a history test? It's not hard to
           guess who her history teacher is.
FRANK   It's me actually ... *(Pause)* ... William the
           Conqueror was also known as the Bastard King.
WINIFRED   Possibly by Irish Republicans, but surely ...
FRANK   No ... no ... that's a fact. Isn't there a Bloody
           Mary?
WINIFRED   How did we get onto drink?
FRANK   No, in history ... she was a person.
WINIFRED   Goodness, I don't remember that from my history.
           (Pause)
FRANK   I had stew on Sunday.
WINIFRED   Pardon?
FRANK   Stew ... a notion I took.
WINIFRED   I had a lovely piece of lamb.
FRANK   Sunday dinner was always an occasion with Isobel.
WINIFRED   You must miss her terribly Frank.
FRANK   Over thirty years together. You get used to being on
           your own. Yes, I get lonely, but for a person, not just
           for company.
WINIFRED   It's not too late for you yet. There's still time to find
           someone to share things with.
FRANK   I see no prospect of that. *(Stopping at a book)* Look at
           this ... "Where was the Battle of the Boyne fought?"
           Answer, "Sandy Row". *(Throwing the books aside)*
WINIFRED   It's odd too ... here we are the best of friends in here.
           Yet we both go home to lonely big houses.
FRANK   I started the bathroom on Sunday morning. I'll do the

110

	whole place, room by room. We always used to do it every three years ... it's nearly seven now. I'll never forget it. I was just finishing the hall door. She called me for a cup of coffee ... when I went in there she was.
WINIFRED	Seven years ... dear oh dear ... doesn't it fly. *(Pause)* I wish I'd someone like you around. That working kitchen of mine's a mess. *(Pause)* I don't suppose ... *(The door opens and Tony enters ... to Frank's relief)*
TONY	Good morning, Winifred ... Frank.
FRANK	Morning, Tony.
WINIFRED	It's very cold, isn't it, Tony?
TONY	There's a very cold wind. *(He removes some books from his briefcase)*
WINIFRED	I didn't think you took work home with you, Tony?
TONY	Not as a rule. This is a few of my O Level lot ... they've been slipping so I set them an extra homework essay.
WINIFRED	Then ruined your weekend marking it?
TONY	No, a couple of hours spread over Friday and Saturday. I had a very pleasant weekend. We went for a drive after church yesterday morning. Saturday evening I spent putting up shelves for Agnes.
WINIFRED	All you busy men ... I feel quite guilty by comparison. Frank spent most of his weekend on the bathroom.
TONY	*(To Frank)* Really ... were you ill?
FRANK	No ... no, decorating.
WINIFRED	I'm just saying I wish I had a man to do my working kitchen for me.
TONY	I'm sure you could get a couple of our fifth-form lads to do it ... for a small consideration.
WINIFRED	Have you taken leave of your senses? Do you seriously think I'd let any of that lot into my home? Huh, if they discovered I was living there on my own ... well ... goodness knows what they'd get up to.
FRANK	That was a bad accident up your direction on Saturday, Tony?
TONY	Yes, the woman's dead apparently, and the child is critical.
WINIFRED	I heard that on the news, what happened?
TONY	It appears an army truck was racing to an explosion and went on through a red light.
WINIFRED	Isn't that dreadful. What's the point of rushing to an explosion to save lives, if you're going to kill half-a-dozen people on the way there?

111

FRANK	They are pretty awful bloody drivers.
WINIFRED	I'll never forget the frosty morning the truck pulled out in front of me ...
	(David crashes into the room, making the others start. He is a tall, powerfully built, good-looking man in his early thirties. He closes the door behind him with a bang)
DAVID	Good morning all. May God bless this school and all fools who fail in her.
TONY	*(As Frank grunts at David)* Good morning, David.
DAVID	Were you old timers re-living your wild weekend? *(Realising that Winifred hasn't greeted him)* Morning, Fred. *(She glares at him)* Sorry ... Winnie.
WINIFRED	Mr Dunn, my name is Winifred or Miss Walker.
DAVID	Well, if you don't know which, how the hell do you expect me to?
WINIFRED	Is it too much to expect you to be civil just one day in your life?
TONY	A good weekend, David?
DAVID	Tone old bone ... what the lads would call a weeker, brill. You should have been with me Winnie-Fred. I was in Dublin. For a pound sterling you can get what the G.I.'s used to get for two bars of chocolate in Saigon. It's a wonderful city ... and for spectacle you can stand at the foot of Nelson's column and watch the punt fall.
WINIFRED	I didn't think Nelson's column was there any more.
DAVID	You jest Winnie, old sport, you jest.
FRANK	*(Deliberately to Winifred)* There's a new statue now, Jim Larkin, the labour leader.
DAVID	Between you and me, old chap, every labour leader this century has been larkin'. *(Pause)* You know, I appreciate that Frankie, old boy. Thought you saw a gap in the old knowledge and tried to fill it. The intellectual's burden and all that. *(Pause)* What do you think of larkin' in O'Connell Street, Tony?
TONY	It's as good a place as any I suppose.
DAVID	What a pun for a Monday morning and him after a weekend's screwing too.
WINIFRED	Really Mr Dunn. I think we could do without your filthy language for one Monday morning.
DAVID	You see, Tony, live on your own and you become preoccupied with sex. I met Tony in a hardware shop on Friday afternoon, buying a selection of screws to put up shelving. You'll be relieved to learn that Agnes

	is still upright and not lying in an exhausted untidy heap.
FRANK	Mr Dunn, you typify what is wrong with this school. It is full of teachers who are living contradictions of the values we are trying to inculcate into the pupils.
WINIFRED	You're not fit to be a teacher.
DAVID	You don't have to be fit . . . sure he's got his heart condition and you've got your headaches. His holiness our headmaster has haemorrhoids, that's why he wears that bloody gown.
WINIFRED	Your kind should be hounded out of the profession.
DAVID	We'd replace you too . . . if we could find someone prepared to do a half day's work, for a whole day's pay.
FRANK	It's time you showed some respect to your elder colleagues.
DAVID	Respect has to be earned, Mercer, old boy. Typical . . . I teach, therefore I deserve respect. What do you say, Tony old chap?
TONY	I think we should put a notice up on the door, "No pupils allowed in the staffroom".
FRANK	He's right.
DAVID	Oh, very droll, old boy, very droll. *(Pause)* *(Herbert Montgomery enters. He is in his fifties and wears a gown. Muttered greetings. All respond except Mr Dunn.)*
HERBERT	I think we'll have someone in for Mr Fleming this afternoon.
WINIFRED	Unless you do something about Mr Dunn, you're going to have to replace the rest of us as well. He'll drive us all into the asylum along with Mr Fleming.
DAVID	All because I wouldn't take her to Dublin for a dirty weekend.
WINIFRED	It's bad enough having to take abuse out there, but in here!
HERBERT	Well, Mr Dunn, you've done it again.
DAVID	Shucks, I can't help it. It must be a natural talent.
FRANK	No sign of an end to the oil strike, Mr Montgomery?
HERBERT	Not a sign. I blame it on the socialists, always wanting more for less.
WINIFRED	I was just saying to Mr Mercer, I'd freeze sooner than see them win.
HERBERT	Indeed, that's the spirit. I'll issue thermal underwear before I'll say die.
FRANK	You've done a wonderful job, Mr Montgomery. You are to be congratulated.

TONY	It is rather uncomfortable in the afternoon though. The girls especially complain of cold.
DAVID	Tell them if they give their sizes at the office, Mr Montgomery will order thermal knickers for them.
TONY	It might be simpler to close an hour earlier.
DAVID	Or take a week off . . . if that wouldn't seem to be copying the intelligent headmasters.
HERBERT	That's one thing about you, Mr Dunn . . . if you know the problem you're never stuck for a drastic solution. *(Pause)* As a matter of fact, Mr Dunn, I'd like a quiet word with you. *(They move down forward. The others occupy themselves)* I've had a complaint from a mother.
DAVID	Does she want to swop her child for one of the school rabbits?
HERBERT	Mrs Dawson is concerned that neither Samuel or Judith have been given homeworks by you lately.
DAVID	There's an excellent reason.
HERBERT	Well, I'd like to know what it is.
DAVID	They're thick, both of them.
HERBERT	Mr Dunn, there is a homework timetable, and they're set homeworks in all their other subjects.
DAVID	Then what's their mother yapping about?
HERBERT	She's "yapping" as you call it, because they have you for history and English and you never set homeworks. '
DAVID	It's a waste of time, theirs and mine. It's time you stopped listening to semi-illiterate parents talking rubbish and paid attention to your staff.
HERBERT	Mr Dunn . . . you are not running this school.
DAVID	Neither are you and that's the problem. I'm not supposed to be running it . . . you are.
HERBERT	How dare you question my integrity.
DAVID	Quite frankly I don't think you have any integrity. *(As Herbert shows concern that the others might overhear)* Oh, don't worry about them. Even if they thought the same as me . . . they'd never have the guts to say it, not to your face anyway
FRANK	Mr Montgomery . . .
HERBERT	It's alright, Frank. I absolutely refuse to be drawn into a slanging match with you, Mr Dunn and I've assured Mrs Dawson that the twins will have homework from now on.
DAVID	That's fine . . . I've no objection at all to you setting them homeworks.
HERBERT	*(Angrily, as David turns away)* Mr Dunn, *(The others look up)* . . . now just you listen to me . . .

114

DAVID	No, you listen to me . . . I'm sick of helping you spread the whitewash over this shithouse. The Dawson twins are thick, both of them. I've been at Wonder Woman there, but she claims they're not remedial.
WINIFRED	The Dawsons are not remedial according to my tests.
DAVID	Screw your tests . . . they're only designed to keep your class numbers down.
HERBERT	You'll regret this, Mr Dunn . . . I can promise you that.
DAVID	Threats . . . rather crude for a headmaster.
HERBERT	I'll be around for quite a while. You might find my good word necessary in the future.
DAVID	That's your problem, isn't it?
HERBERT	Miss Walker . . . Winifred . . . perhaps you'd be good enough to take the Dawson twins under your wing until I sort this out?
WINIFRED	Of course, Mr Montgomery.
HERBERT	Frank, perhaps you'll ensure that Mr Dunn's classes have sufficient history homeworks . . . and will you do the same for English, Tony?
FRANK	With all due respect, Mr Montgomery, I do have my own classes to attend to.
HERBERT	As Head of the History Department, I'd have considered it to be your ultimate responsibility. Setting homeworks isn't a major task.
FRANK	Well, I think it is. The homeworks can only be based on what Mr Dunn is actually doing . . . and besides, what about the marking? I couldn't possibly take on any extra.
TONY	I'll have to agree on that point, Herbert. Extra marking would be impossible. Homework is the responsibility of every individual teacher. We devised the homework timetable on that understanding.
FRANK	Exactly.
HERBERT	It will not have escaped your notice, Mr Dunn, that there is not a single voice to support you in here.
DAVID	I couldn't give a shit.
WINIFRED	Disgusting talk . . .
DAVID	I'm sick asking you to call a staff-meeting to discuss the homework timetable and other issues.
HERBERT	I do not call staff-meetings at your behest.
DAVID	Fair enough, but until you do I will not set homeworks when I believe it to be a waste of time.
HERBERT	I will not submit to blackmail.
WINIFRED	Well said . . . we're all behind you, Mr Montgomery.

115

DAVID	You'll support him all right. There isn't another headmaster in the country who would allow you to sit in here gossiping and sipping tea when you're supposed to be teaching. You should have two timetables, one for your teaching, and one for your headaches.
WINIFRED	How dare you . . .
DAVID	Come on, deny it . . . you're a standing joke in this school.
HERBERT	Miss Walker has given the best years of her life to the teaching profession.
DAVID	Why didn't she do us a favour and give them to some other profession?
FRANK	Damned impertinent pup.
TONY	That's uncalled for, David.
DAVID	If you mean it doesn't need stating because we all know it to be true, I agree.
TONY	It doesn't need stating because you are not in a position to judge the professional competence of any other member of staff. We could all buy popularity by not setting homeworks and holding the school and our colleagues up to ridicule.
DAVID	Homework is a waste of time, Tony, and you know it.
TONY	I know no such thing. I was one of the three departmental heads responsible for drawing up the homework timetable. Frank was another. Of course, there are pupils for whom it is less useful than others. You don't have insights denied the rest of us, but there has to be a system. Your refusal to work, it will not wreck the system, it will merely impose an extra burden on your colleagues. Well, I for one refuse to accept that imposition.
DAVID	*(Glaring at him)* So what do you propose to do about it?
TONY	If you refuse to cooperate with me, I'll refuse to have you in the English Department.
FRANK	The same applies to the History Department . . . you can go back to your headstands and neck-rolls.
HERBERT	I think I'll leave you to sort things out, Tony.
DAVID	Exit Batman.
HERBERT	You were appointed as a PE teacher, Mr Dunn. I think that is worth bearing in mind. *(He goes, pleased)*
DAVID	*(Seething)* That should have increased your stock, Tony. He'll wear his bedroom slippers when it's your turn for a kick on the balls. *(Pause)*
TONY	Do you set any English homeworks at all, David?

116

DAVID	*(Sullen)* A few, when I think they're necessary.
TONY	Well, I'd like you to set them when *I* think they're necessary. That is, in accordance with the homework timetable.
DAVID	I've no fight with you, Tony, but I'm going to get that old bollocks Montgomery.
TONY	I'm not interested in that. I took you into the English Department on condition that you fitted in.
DAVID	So you think that homeworks are wonderful?
TONY	If you want to discuss the merits of homework with me, fine ... but it has to be a serious discussion. Being able to shout louder than anyone else doesn't give your point of view greater validity.
DAVID	How can even you justify the setting of homeworks just as a matter of course. For pupils who can barely read or write? It's all a show for parents.
TONY	There are serious problems we all admit that.
DAVID	His Holiness doesn't ... *(Points at Frank)* ... he doesn't ... *(Points at Winifred)* ... she doesn't. I've been at her for months about the Dawson twins.
WINIFRED	I've told you already, Mr Dunn ...
DAVID	Never mind the Mr Dunn bit. The Dawson's are not capable of doing any meaningful work ... in my book that makes them remedial.
WINIFRED	Huh, I think you want to shove the burden of your work onto me, so that you have more time to go off gallivanting to Dublin. Maybe if you'd spent more time at home, your marriage wouldn't have broken down.
DAVID	Go on, you fucking old reprobate ...
TONY	David, for crying out loud ...
FRANK	Wonderful language. ... You should be round at the incinerator cadging cigarettes with the rest of the thugs.
DAVID	Someday those thugs might discover how you've conned them ... then they'll feed you into that bloody incinerator.
FRANK	I've conned nobody. It's through the efforts of the likes of me that pups like you ever made it to this side of the staffroom door.
DAVID	So I'm your token nigger ... what do you want, a medal ... or will you settle for a bottle of scotch? *(Pause)*
FRANK	I will not have you in my department any more Mr Dunn. I will not tolerate you any longer. *(Exit)*
TONY	Congratulations, David. Personal insults are not going

117

	to make any impact on the serious problems we do have to face.
DAVID	Personal insults? Will you tell me what my marriage has to do with that old bitch.
TONY	Will you please stop your corner-boy language?
DAVID	Is that what it is . . . and how the hell would you know that? It would take a Charles bloody Darwin to convince you that the people you teach belong to the same species as yourself.
TONY	Come on now, this is absolutely futile. Let's just all calm down.
DAVID	Just lift the corner of the carpet, sweep it all under. *(Frank returns)*
FRANK	*(To David)* Did you return the projector on Friday, Mr Dunn?
DAVID	I didn't borrow it on Friday.
FRANK	I know . . . you borrowed it on Wednesday and failed to return it.
DAVID	Ah yes. *(To Winifred)* I was showing a blue movie.
FRANK	That wouldn't surprise me.
DAVID	Right enough, I suppose you've seen them all.
FRANK	Maybe you'll bring it up with you at break . . . I'd like to use it before lunch.
DAVID	I'll send it round. I don't want you humping it around, not with your bad heart and all. *(Frank Grunts, lifts his flask and leaves)* The flask, that's what he really came back for. Nothing like the old Brooke Bond and Bushmills.
WINIFRED	You can gloat, but then you'll never know the loss of a mate of over thirty years standing.
DAVID	Remind me to order some violins for the school band. I must have a pee. *(David exit)*
WINIFRED	He's terribly coarse. *(Fade lights)*

SCENE 5

	(David in his classroom. Maureen and Ann are with him)
DAVID	You two stand there, I'll deal with you in a minute. *(He perches on his desk to address the class)* Back to what I was at yesterday. I think myself Anthony was a bit wet ... like you McDonald. Manchester United's win on Saturday doesn't justify this degree of frivolity, son. The first four goals were offside. *(Pause)* All right ... settle down. I'm a Cleopatra fan myself. Mind you ... if she'd had that old barge on the Lagan I'd have taught her a trick or two. You may smile, Mandy ... I mean it. Now, I think Cleo was a great character ... but I don't want you to tell me what I think. I want to know what you think. Bear in mind though ... whatever opinions you offer must be backed up from the text. Find suitable quotations and use them effectively. *(Pause)* Right ... get on with it, quietly. *(Pause. Looking at Maureen and Ann)* Now you two ... *(He moves round and sits behind the desk)* Maureen ... *(Picking up a notebook)* ... I'll have you first. Pull that chair over. *(She does so)* The rest of you just attend to your own work. *(Pause. With a notebook)* This isn't very good, is it?
MAUREEN	No, sir.
DAVID	No, sir ... and why not, madam? *(Pause. She looks very sheepish and then appears close to tears)* Tears aren't going to help, young lady ... I want an explanation. You obviously didn't bother to read the book.
MAUREEN	It's my granny, sir.
DAVID	Your granny ...? *(Touching her hand as tears come, much softer)* take your time and don't be crying ... what's wrong with your granny?
MAUREEN	She's sick you see, sir and I have to go round and look after her.
DAVID	You have to ... why is that?
MAUREEN	I have to make her dinner and all, sir, and clean up. You see she won't leave her own house or anything and she's afraid of them sending her to hospital.
DAVID	What about your mother?
MAUREEN	She works all day and then I've two wee brothers and a wee sister.
DAVID	Is your father at home?
MAUREEN	*(Pause)* No, sir ... he's away ... in jail.

119

DAVID	I see . . . I always loved my grannies, so I can understand you wanting to help yours . . . in fact I think it's greatly to your credit that you do. On the other hand, I'm sure your granny would like you to do well at school, wouldn't she?
MAUREEN	Yes, sir.
DAVID	O Levels aren't going to get you to heaven, Maureen, but they might be useful. You have the ability and you have to be at school . . . so you should try and get as much out of it as you possibly can. Don't you agree?
MAUREEN	Yes, sir . . . I'll try, sir.
DAVID	That's the spirit. I'll tell you what I'll do . . . I'll work out a special timetable for you. You can work on your own in class . . . and at home when you have the chance. You can do it . . . but only if you stop worrying. If you'd explained all this to me earlier we could easily have sorted it out. Can you come and see me for half an hour after school on Wednesday?
MAUREEN	Yes, sir . . . thank you, sir.
DAVID	Right . . . back to your seat and we'll say no more about it. *(She goes. David sits thoughtfully)* Ann Wilson . . . up here. Get your horrible snout back into that book, Gore . . . otherwise my little bamboo asp will be stinging you. *(Ann Wilson sits. She is small, heavily made up, with large earrings in pierced ears. Nice looking, confident and cheeky)* We're only reading this play, Ann . . . we're not casting it.
ANN	What do you mean, sir?
DAVID	Never mind. You're not allowed to wear flamboyant earrings.
ANN	They're not flamboyant . . . they're real gold.
DAVID	You know the rules on earrings.
ANN	I couldn't find any studs, sir and I'm afraid of my holes closing.
DAVID	Are you chewing?
ANN	It's special, sir, out of the chemists, for bad breath.
DAVID	Put it in the basket.
ANN	Ach, sir . . .
DAVID	The basket . . .
ANN	*(Swallowing hard)* I've swallowed it, sir.
DAVID	You know, if I had a stomach pump, I'd teach you a lesson about obedience. *(Referring to her book)* A trifle short, wouldn't you say? *(To Class)* Jones . . . sit round . . . get on with it. *(Pause. To Ann)* Well?
ANN	That's all I could think of, sir.
DAVID	Have you read the book?

120

ANN	Yes, sir.
DAVID	Nearly two hundred pages and you can only manage twenty-two lines?
ANN	I was rushing, sir.
DAVID	Obviously . . . why?
ANN	Well, you see, sir, I was kneeling on the kitchen table and my da needed it to paste the paper on.
DAVID	Paste the paper on?
ANN	Yes, sir, he was papering our living-room.
DAVID	Didn't you tell him you had homework to do?
ANN	Aye . . . he told me to clear off or he'd paste me as well.
DAVID	Do you want to do this exam, Ann?
ANN	*(Shrugs)* I suppose so.
DAVID	Don't do us any favours, dear. It doesn't matter to me, you know. I have my degree . . . I'm capable of earning a living. If working is too much trouble for you, I'm sure we can find you a place in the dole queue.
ANN	I do want to do it sir . . . my ma says I have to.
DAVID	Right . . . tomorrow afternoon, half past three, you be here . . . and you can start again. *(As she goes surlily)* Rest assured I'll not be papering the staffroom.
TONY	*(Rapping and entering)* Excuse me, David. Could I have a word with them?
DAVID	Sure . . . *(Rising and coming round the desk)* . . . Right you horrible shower, pay attention to Mr Cairns.
TONY	*(Waiting for complete quiet)* Come on, pens down . . . you, you, waken up lad. *(Pause)* Now, Mrs Wylie has organised a trip to the theatre . . . and there are some seats left. Hands up anyone who is interested in going. *(Every hand goes up)* Goodness . . . you must have this lot inspired, Mr Dunn.
DAVID	Don't you believe it. *(To class)* The visit is after school, in the evening. *(Pause)* Seven.
TONY	She can only take another four.
DAVID	*(To class)* It costs a quid. *(Pause)* Three. Girls . . . wouldn't you know?
TONY	Right . . . will you scribble their names down for Mrs Wylie . . . and if you can coax another one.
DAVID	*(To Class)* That's it . . . the commercial's over, back to work. *(Pause. Quietly to Tony)* I'll talk to young Maureen Baxter . . . I'll pay for her. *(Tony looks at him)* Problems at home. I'll tell you later.
TONY	*(Going)* Good . . . I'll see you at lunch.

DAVID	Right . . . *(Going with him to the door)* . . . Tony . . . about this morning . . .
TONY	You've a lot to offer these kids, David, I've always known that. You shouldn't let your personal vendetta with Montgomery come between you and them.
DAVID	I know I went over the top . . .
TONY	We're all aware of the problems . . . and despite appearances at times, I think we're all trying to address ourselves to them. *(Pause)* Anyway, I'll see you at lunch. *(Goes. David, thoughtful, returns to his desk)* *(Fade lights)*

SCENE 6

(Cairns' classroom. It contains cleaning equipment . . . mops, buckets, etc. Allen and Boyd enter and knock)

TONY	Come in. *(They enter)*
ALLEN	Hello, sir.
TONY	*(Stands)* Well, well, well. It's Allen, isn't it? Allen and Boyd?
ALLEN	Tom Allen, sir.
BOYD	Bill Boyd . . . Mr Cairns.
TONY	Come in, come in, pull out a couple of chairs.
ALLEN	We're not disturbing you, sir?
TONY	Not at all, not at all. No, I'm always pleased to see old boys. No, I'm just marking the inevitable pile of homeworks. *(Pause)* So what brings you two back up here?
BOYD	Just passing, thought we'd drop in like.
TONY	What are you doing with yourselves now?
BOYD	I'm still on the dole, haven't had a job yet.
TONY	Really, you're out over two years, aren't you?
BOYD	Aye, but the oul jobs are scarce.
TONY	What about you . . . Tom?
BOYD	Jerry.
ALLEN	I'm on the dole too. I had a job but . . .
BOYD	He got the boot.
TONY	Really, what happened?
ALLEN	Ah . . . *(Dirty look at Boyd)* . . . just a wee bit of bother, sir.
BOYD	He stuck one on the foreman.

122

ALLEN	*(Nudging Boyd)* It was nothing, sir. Just a bit of an argument.
TONY	I see, and what was the job?
ALLEN	It was just labouring, up in Mackies.
TONY	Striking the foreman . . .
BOYD	Kicked him in so he did.
TONY	. . . That's not going to look good on your record.
ALLEN	He said something to me. I just lost the head.
TONY	And the job. How long had you worked there?
ALLEN	Just over a year. *(Pause)* He said things about my sister.
BOYD	He used to sing a wee song about her. Tell him about that, Jerry.
ALLEN	It's just daft. He used to sort of chant it every time he passed me. *(Cairns waits)* "Your sister's shit, 'cause she's married to a Brit, Do Da, Do Da".
BOYD	He was a Mick. Jerry just spread him.
ALLEN	*(Threateningly to Boyd)* Why don't you shut up?
TONY	Now lads, that's enough. *(Pause)* Why do they call you Jerry?
BOYD	Tom and Jerry on the telly.
ALLEN	It's not that. It used to be TA, you know the territorials. Then Big Skinso Andrews started calling me Terry for short. Somebody made a mistake, some thickie, like him.
BOYD	All right, Mastermind. I'm Scout, 'cause my initials are BB, you know, Boys Brigade.
ALLEN	It is not, it's because you always wanted to be the scout when we played cowboys and Indians.
BOYD	Naw it wasn't.
ALLEN	It was because I was the one who started it.
BOYD	Aye, wise it, son. Whose nickname is it?
TONY	All right, lads. So, you're both unemployed . . . any plans?
ALLEN	I was thinking of joining the Merchant Navy, sir, see a bit of the world. But it's the oul lad . . . he's bad again.
BOYD	John Wayne had that, but he went on making pictures.
ALLEN	John Wayne had cancer, my da hasn't got cancer and he's not a film star.
BOYD	That was even worse then . . . but he still acted.
ALLEN	It was not worse, you're a walking mouth, son. You can jump on and off horses with cancer, you couldn't with a bad heart.
BOYD	You can have it anywhere. You could even have it in

123

	the ... bum ... you couldn't have jumped on and off a horse with it there.
ALLEN	Aye, well, that shows how much you know, John Wayne didn't have it there.
BOYD	It can even be in breasts.
ALLEN	Fade out, son, imagine John Wayne with cancer of the ...
TONY	Yes, yes ... I'd forgotten about your father. Is he at home now?
ALLEN	No, he's been in for about four weeks. He's having another big operation soon. He's in and out all the time.
TONY	Who looks after him when he's at home?
ALLEN	He won't let anybody in, I have to now that Norma's married.
TONY	Yes, of course, she married a soldier.
BOYD	"Shit, shit, she married a Brit."
ALLEN	You say that again, son, I'll kick your head in.
BOYD	Aye, you and what navy?
TONY	Boyd! What about Joe?
ALLEN	He's inside, fourteen years for armed robbery. There's just me and my da ... when he's at home.
TONY	Armed robbery ... was anyone shot?
ALLEN	A clerk just got hit in the shoulder. He was trying to get himself a medal. You'd have thought it was his money they wanted.
TONY	A clerk ... was it a bank?
ALLEN	Aye, up in Antrim.
TONY	I taught Joe.
BOYD	You've taught our whole family. Brenda's still here. Do you have her this year?
TONY	Yes, I've had her right through.
BOYD	She's a right wee bitch, isn't she?
TONY	She's not very interested in working.
BOYD	She hates school. So did I. Our whole family hated it.
TONY	Patricia liked it. She could have gone on, like Tom there. She could have done O Levels.
BOYD	She's married now. Has a ba.
TONY	Married, with a baby! But she only left a year ago.
BOYD	It only takes nine months nowadays.
	(Pause)
BOYD	Ponge Edgar knocked her up the shoot, they'd a wee boy. George Carl Edgar.
TONY	Ernie Edgar.
BOYD	Pongo Edgar, but I kicked him in for it.
TONY	Ernie Edgar and Patricia. None of the girls would go

124

	near him, he stank. Patricia and ... I can't ... she was bright and beautiful.
BOYD	And drunk on the eleventh night.
TONY	Ernie Edgar could barely read or write.
ALLEN	You don't have to sign for that, sir.
TONY	I coaxed her from third form. She was one of the brightest girls I ever taught ... Pongo Edgar ... she's lucky she didn't catch foot and mouth disease being that close to him. What did your parents say?
BOYD	The oul lad's dead. My ma give off a bit. It's one of those things, isn't it?
TONY	One of those things! No, it isn't one of those things. It's a disgrace, a waste. Does he work?
BOYD	He sweeps the roads. The money's not bad.
TONY	A road sweeper, and she had so much potential. Does she work?
BOYD	Naw, sure she's got the ba. She's a dirty bitch now. The whole house is rotten and the ba's stinking all the time. She doesn't change it often enough and it gets that nappy rash. Its arse is all big red sores.
TONY	I really thought Patricia was something special.
BOYD	Here, did you fancy her yourself?
TONY	Don't be ridiculous.
BOYD	Do you but, I mean some of the girls?
TONY	Boyd, I'm a very happily married man. I have a daughter of my own, and I'm certainly not interested in schoolgirls.
ALLEN	Some of the girls used to fancy you, sir.
TONY	Be that as it may, I can assure you that it was never reciprocated. *(Pause)* That means I never fancied them in return, Boyd.
BOYD	Oh . . . it was Dunn they all fancied. It used to be up on the walls, "Nancy Moore's been done by Dunn". I'm not joking, that's what it said. He was the pin-up ... wasn't that right, Jerry? *(Pause)* Most of the girls in this school are bats anyway. *(Pause)*
ALLEN	Ah . . . a lot of girls are like that, sir, as soon as they get married they let themselves go.
TONY	I suppose they feel it's hopeless and just give up. Married to people like Pongo Edgar I'm not surprised.
BOYD	I wouldn't even take a cup of tea in our Patricia's. *(Pause)*
ALLEN	*(Glancing at an open door)* I see you're still doing the oul War Poets, sir.
TONY	What? ... Yes, still ... the War Poets. They seem to go down well.

125

BOYD	Oul Winifred Owens . . . I never liked her.
TONY	Wilfred Owens, *he* was killed a week before the armistice.
BOYD	Was he a boy? I never liked poetry. All poets are tootie fruities.
TONY	I think that observation would amuse Lord Byron.
ALLEN	Pay no attention to him, sir. My best one was Rupert Brooke: "If I should die, think only this of me; That there's some corner of a foreign field That is forever England".
TONY	I'm delighted that you have remembered something.
ALLEN	You slapped me round the head one day and made me copy that poem out twenty times. *(Pause)*
TONY	You were lazy, Tom. It used to anger me. You could have been good. You could have been doing A Levels now.
ALLEN	I might have just struggled through a couple and then what?
TONY	Then university or teacher training college. You gave up without even trying.
ALLEN	Who'd look after the oul fella?
TONY	You can't afford to squander your chances to look after a sick relative.
ALLEN	My da's dying, any minute he could go.
TONY	There are people trained and paid to look after the sick.
ALLEN	My da doesn't want strangers looking after him . . . neither do I.
TONY	You told me you wanted to leave school and get a job because the money was needed at home. Now what are you doing?
ALLEN	It's not that easy, sir.
TONY	Nothing is that easy, but that is what you are looking for. You're looking for the easy way. If you had stuck at it Norma would have had to look after your father for a bit longer.
ALLEN	Norma was seven months pregnant when she got married.
TONY	Another casualty of war?
BOYD	That's the Brits for you. If it moves and wears trousers they shoot it. If it moves and wears a skirt they screw it . . . sorry.
TONY	*(Nastily)* Pongo Edgar wasn't a Brit.
BOYD	Pongo Edgar's a shit.
TONY	I just don't understand you lads.

126

ALLEN	I don't know how you stuck us, sir. I couldn't do it. We only worked when we wanted to.
TONY	You always . . . nearly always worked for me.
ALLEN	We did more work for you, and Mr Dunn, than for any of the others . . . that's because you two used to knock us about. You know, we used to sit around and decide which teachers to rake on which days. You used to try hard and we worked a bit for you, but we didn't care.
TONY	Labouring in Mackies is not the way out, Tom.
ALLEN	The way out for me's through the City Cemetery, when the oul lad snuffs it.
BOYD	I'd like out too, I'm going to try for the oil rigs, it's great money.
ALLEN	They'd know you were the Irishman, because you'd be throwing bread to the helicopters.
BOYD	Aye, I know, did you steal that out of a Christmas cracker?
TONY	What about your brothers, Boyd?
BOYD	Mark's in the police, but I'm too thick for that. Sammy's in the army, but I'm not that thick. The oil rigs, that's where the money is.
TONY	Have you written away, have you applied?
ALLEN	Don't encourage him, sir.
BOYD	The oil rigs is definitely the place. You get piles of money and there's nowhere to spend it. Home for a couple of weeks every few months, loaded.
TONY	There's more to life than money, Boyd.
BOYD	Does your wife work?
TONY	She teaches in a primary school.
BOYD	That's handy like, for money. My oul woman works in a laundry. *(Pause)* Do you have kids?
TONY	I have two, a boy and a girl.
ALLEN	Did they do their A Levels, sir?
TONY	You know, Allen, you're civil to the point of insolence. *(Pause)* Yes . . . they did. Matthew is at Oxford, he's an historian. Elizabeth is doing medicine at Queens.
ALLEN	What did you have in mind for me, sir?
TONY	Sarcasm is hardly called for.
ALLEN	The oul fella'd never have agreed to me going away to Oxford. Mind you, medicine's handy.
BOYD	Do you need A Levels for the oil rigs?
TONY	I'd hardly think so for what you'll be doing on them. *(Pause)*
ALLEN	Do you like teaching, sir?

127

TONY	It can be interesting, rewarding. It's good to see young people going on and doing something with their lives.
ALLEN	Did any of our lot go on?
TONY	Yes, as a matter of fact, two or three. Paul Martin did. There were two of the girls, Betty Armstrong and the Woods girl.
ALLEN	Jean Woods.
BOYD	She goes with a soldier.
TONY	She's hoping to do English at university.
BOYD	That's if the Brit doesn't do her first . . .
TONY	You could have been doing the same, Allen. So could Roy Alexander.
BOYD	Roy's up in . . .
ALLEN	*(Cutting in quickly)* He did O Levels.
TONY	Yes, he did extremely well too. He passed five, three with top grades. He had to drop out though, there were problems at home. I think his parents were breaking up.
BOYD	His da's living with a barmaid. You want to see her. Tell him what she's like, Jerry.
ALLEN	She's not as nice now as she was when she worked in the bar.
TONY	What is Roy doing now?
BOYD	Roy Alexander?
ALLEN	*(Nudging him)* He's never around now. Skinso Andrews joined the army. He only stuck it about four months. The twins went to Australia.
BOYD	I might try Australia, after the oil rigs. Save a few bob, buy a sheep farm.
TONY	I've a sister in Australia. She lectures in a university there. We were out visiting her a few years ago.
ALLEN	I don't fancy it. *(Pause)*
BOYD	Are there any new teachers now?
TONY	We've a couple of new men . . . and a very attractive new English teacher, Miss Lindsay.
BOYD	Hey, Hey, an English teacher.
TONY	Boyd, calm down. Mr Talbot has left, so has Miss Dunbar.
ALLEN	Talbot? Do you remember the day Pongo brought his da up? Up comes his oul fella, all the gear, combat jacket, big army boots, studded belt . . . Talbot kicked his light in. *(Allen and Boyd laugh)* It's the only time in my life I nearly liked Talbot.
BOYD	Ernie's da.
ALLEN/ BOYD	Superpong.

128

BOYD	Did you ever kick anybody's da in?
TONY	I don't believe in violence.
ALLEN	You used to slap me around all the time, sir.
TONY	That wasn't violence, that was psychology. I was trying to convince you that you had ability.
BOYD	You used to cane me all the time.
TONY	I was trying to convince you that lack of ability was no excuse for lack of effort. I assumed you enjoyed it, you kept coming back for more. Victor Hill was another. I must have caned you pair at least once a day. *(Pause)*
BOYD	Victor's dead now.
TONY	What happened to him?
BOYD	He stepped out of line, so they plugged him.
ALLEN	You don't know who done it.
BOYD	Everybody knows who done it.
ALLEN	He asked ror it.
TONY	How did he step out of line? What did he do? *(Pause)*
ALLEN	He squealed to the cops, so they shot him. He couldn't keep his mouth shut.
TONY	*(Angry at Allen's obvious lack of sympathy)* How do you know he "squealed"? How do you know? Did someone tell you it was him and you just accepted that?
ALLEN	Take it easy, sir, I didn't shoot him. He made a statement ... it was read out.
BOYD	Anybody could have writ that.
ALLEN	Why don't you keep your mouth shut?
TONY	Where did it happen? Did you see it?
BOYD	We all seen it. We were taken to see it. It was a lesson, a warning to the rest of us.
TONY	So you're all in it?
ALLEN	We're not in nothing.
TONY	So why were you taken to see the murder of one of your school friends?
ALLEN	He was no friend of mine.
TONY	You went about with him here. I used to see you together all the time.
ALLEN	We were in the same smoking group that's all.
TONY	You knew him. How could you sit and watch that? *(Pause)* How did they do it?
BOYD	It was good.
TONY	Good! It was good? You sat and watched a young fellow of your own age being murdered, shot dead, and you are saying it was good?
ALLEN	He doesn't mean what you think. He means the way

129

	they did it he didn't have a chance. There was no messing.
TONY	When did it happen? I don't remember it in the papers.
ALLEN	There's that many, you probably just didn't notice.
TONY	I taught him for four years, everyday for four years. Of course, I'd have noticed. I must have been away, when did it happen?
ALLEN	Last year sometime.
TONY	When? Summer? . . . Winter? . . . when?
ALLEN	I'm not sure, I think it was August.
TONY	August . . . I was away. Yes, we toured the South. *(Pause)* What was it like? I'm not acting schoolmaster . . . but to have sat there . . . what was it like? *(Pause)*
BOYD	They just tied him . . .
ALLEN	Look, sir . . . they shot him for informing.
TONY	No, no, I don't want you to inform. I don't want names or addresses . . . just describe how it happened . . . please . . . *(Pause)*
ALLEN	There's this hut round our way. It's a sort of a club. We were all told to go there one night. There's a platform, just like in the Assembly Hall and we were all told to sit down. There were five or six men and two women on the platform. They all wore hoods and combat jackets and things. One of the men got up and started talking. He talked about the struggle and how they were fighting and risking their lives for us. He read out a list of men and women in the area who'd died for the cause. Then he started about traitors and informers. They brought Victor in. *(Pause)* He was tied up and gagged. They had to sort of drag him in, and even though he was gagged you could still hear him sobbing. *(Pause)* There was a chair . . . they tied him into it. Then the man read out a statement Victor'd made. You could see his eyes, all puffed up and red. When that man had finished reading, another came forward, with one of the women. The man had a gun. The woman had a big towel. She wrapped the towel round his head . . . and then the man . . . twice. *(Pause)* There was silence and they dragged him out, chair and all. Suddenly the noise started . . . everybody just talking . . . and . . . laughing. People were laughing and imitating the way his head had jerked and rolled. It was nerves, you could tell. When we went out we just hung about for a long time . . . but I don't think anybody spoke. *(Long pause)*

TONY	The men he's supposed to have informed on, what happened to them? *(Pause)*
ALLEN	There were three of them . . . two of them got ten years and the one who's supposed to have fired the gun got fourteen.
TONY	I see . . . Has anyone been caught for the murder?
ALLEN	The police aren't going to get excited about an inside one. They'd be happy if they all wiped each other out.
TONY	You tell me you're not involved, then why did they want you to see it?
ALLEN	Who is or isn't involved when you live in the middle of it?
TONY	There's a confidential telephone system. You could write anonymous letters. If you really wanted to, you could have a lot of them put away.
ALLEN	What would we do that for?
TONY	What do you mean? They're killers, gangsters.
ALLEN	What would happen if we did that? Suppose we got every last one of them put away, then what?
TONY	Then we'd have peace. Decent people would be able to get on with leading normal lives.
BOYD	Aye, right enough. Them other bastards would come over and wipe us out.
TONY	I mean we have all to get involved . . . on both sides.
BOYD	Aye, well let them start.
ALLEN	It's like the Yanks and the Russians, sir.
TONY	If we start putting our house in order . . . the police and the army will protect us.
BOYD	The police and the army! They might protect you lot, they wouldn't protect us. Anyway, you can't squeal, no way.
TONY	It is not squealing or informing, or whatever you like to call it, it is self-defence.
BOYD	Keeping your mouth shut's self-defence.
ALLEN	My brother's doing fourteen years because of an informer.
TONY	For armed robbery and for shooting someone.
ALLEN	He's still my brother.
TONY	Is he, even when he does that? Suppose he'd killed the clerk?
ALLEN	So what? The stupid frigger should have minded his own business.
TONY	That was his business. It is everybody's business. Did we not teach you that much here?
ALLEN	I'll tell you what you taught me here, sir. You taught me that you work hardest for the people who hit you

	the hardest. The hard men are the ones you don't mess about. They're the ones you keep quiet for.
TONY	Is that the sum total of all my efforts?
ALLEN	Comprehension and the War Poets count for nothing out there.
TONY	What about Joe, does he feel it was worth it now?
ALLEN	Nothing ever seems worth it when you're caught, but there are hundreds who've never been caught and never will be.
BOYD	It's not us anyway . . . we never bother.
ALLEN	We just mind our own business, sir, it's the only way. *(Pause)*
TONY	How did your father take it when Joe was put away?
ALLEN	What's it matter to the oul fella? He'll not be around in fourteen years.
TONY	Didn't it upset him?
ALLEN	I don't know.
TONY	Did he not say anything? Did he not seem hurt?
ALLEN	How would you know what's hurting him?
TONY	How long has your mother been dead?
ALLEN	My ma's not dead, no such luck.
TONY	I'm sorry, I thought . . . sorry. I should have remembered. You lose track, there are so many.
ALLEN	It's all right, sir. It doesn't bother me now. *(Pause)* Do you never get tired marking them oul homeworks, sir?
TONY	Yes, constantly, but it has to be done.
BOYD	It's a bit thick, just don't give any homework and then you'll not have to mark it.
TONY	It's important to set homework. It's important for pupils to learn to work on their own, to find things out for themselves. It's also important because we don't have enough time in class to do all we have to do.
BOYD	Oul Ma Mairs used to put the Maths homework on the board, answers and all. We just had to copy it down.
TONY	She put the answers on the board?
BOYD	Aye, just toul us to copy it rough and then copy it out again neatly at home. My ma used to do mine all the time.
TONY	That's most irregular. What is the point of giving you homework . . . Well, perhaps she had her own reasons.
ALLEN	It looked good in the homework books . . . and it was our reward for being good. Wee Roy complained about her. Said she wasn't teaching him anything.

132

BOYD	Skinso kicked him in for that.
TONY	Roy was very keen. It's a great pity about him.
BOYD	It was his own fault. Everybody knew he was doing it ... he was warned to go into hiding before that last one.
TONY	What are you talking about?
ALLEN	D'you see you, Boyd, you've got a mouth like bloody Portsmouth.
TONY	Do you mean Roy's in trouble as well? *(Pause)*
BOYD	I thought you knew, you said it was a great pity about him.
TONY	I meant it was a pity he had to give up school because he was such a very good lad. *(Pause)*
ALLEN	What big mouth means is that Wee Roy was one of the top hit men ... he's doing four life-sentences for murders.
TONY	Roy Alexander? Is this a stupid joke? You are telling me that Roy, one of the quietest boys in this school ...
ALLEN	What's quiet go to do with it? Where did you spend the summer, sir, the South of Ireland or the South Pole?
TONY	I remember it now. Of course I read it, but ... it didn't seem possible. Even now it seems preposterous. I remarked on the name to my wife ... when she said it was probably the same one, I could have laughed at the very idea of it. Roy Alexander! *(Pause)* So he killed Victor Hill?
ALLEN	No, he did not.
TONY	No, he did not! You know it all. You know who killed and who didn't kill, who robbed and who didn't rob. You know that "stupid friggers" deserve to be shot in the shoulder ... and if they happen to be killed it's their own fault. You know everything ... Let me tell you something, Allen ... if I thought ... if I thought Alexander did it, I'd inform on him myself. Yes, I'd be go to the police ... they could slap another life sentence on him.
ALLEN	Well, he didn't.
TONY	How can you be so damned sure he didn't?
ALLEN	Because I was there. Because they brought someone in to do it. Because he was twice as tall and three times as broad as Roy. Because Roy was already in custody when it happened. *(Pause)* If you'd stop reading them fancy English papers, you'd maybe know what was going on. They don't know about us in *The Guardian* or *The Sunday Times*. They don't wont to know. Unless you

	kick your dog, or screw your local princess, you don't make the front page. We're just loyalist extremists. We're never right, we're never reasonable and we're never recognised. We're just a mass of extremists from West Belfast and they think that stretches from the Mourne Mountains to the Giant's Causeway. They think there are a million of us swarming all over the place, smothering all the wee innocent Catholics. But there aren't. There's a handful of us, and we're just fighting to survive.
TONY	To survive . . . to survive what?
ALLEN	Just to survive. It's those other bastards who're doing it all. They're doing all the murdering and blowing up factories. Look at me, do I look like a rich, influential member of the Protestant ascendancy? I've got nothing . . . I live in a slum . . . I can't get a job . . . I've no fancy car . . . my ma ran off with her fancyman . . . my sister got knocked up the shoot by a Brit . . . my brother's in jail . . . and my da's dying in agony. *(Pause)* Now you go out on to the Falls Road and see how many of the poor underprivileged minority want to change places with me.
TONY	So you are involved?
ALLEN	Yes, I am involved. After considering the endless list of opportunities I decided I'd better stick with my own people, in my own area and just fight to survive. I do as little as possible. I'm lucky 'cause the oul lad's always a good excuse to get out of things . . . and as soon as he goes, I'm getting right out. *(Pause)*
BOYD	You used to bring us in the coloured books out of them fancy papers. I remember one day you caned me and Hillso 'cause we were looking at a woman with a big pair of headlights. Imagine caning us and they were your dirty books. *(Pause)*
TONY	What did Alexander do?
BOYD	He shot four Fenians.
TONY	Fenians! What do you know about Fenians? You're just an ignorant cliche-sprouting cornerboy . . . a lout. You dismiss them as if they were dried fish.
ALLEN	They were IRA men.
TONY	They are always IRA men. Every Roman Catholic in Ireland is an IRA man according to you lot.
ALLEN	Well, they bloody well are.
TONY	Don't you swear at me, Allen.
ALLEN	I'm not in school now, sir.
TONY	You are in school. You may not be a pupil, but you

	are in school. I'm still a teacher and I demand some respect.
ALLEN	That's all you ever cared about. As long as we could say, "Yes, sir ... no sir ... three bags full, sir". Nothing else mattered.
BOYD	You used to hit me for not saying "sir" . . . sir. *(Pause)*
TONY	Roy Alexander. When I think of the hours I spent with him in the staffroom. God help me in my innocence. I even offered to go to his house and give him extra tuition. I could have given you dozens of names of boys I would have thought were capable of that sort of thing, but not Roy. He wasn't tough, was he?
ALLEN	You don't have to be tough, just mad enough. Some of the toughest ones I know couldn't kill anyone.
TONY	You say he got life?
BOYD	I heard he's good living now . . . sings hymns all the time.
ALLEN	The judge said that in his case life should mean life. *(Pause)*
TONY	He'll have time to do his 'A' Levels now. We seem to have created an obscene, perverted new system of higher education. *(Pause)* You lot spend ten years in school and most of you can't wait to get out. Then as soon as you're out you just throw away the rest of your lives.
ALLEN	You just get involved.
BOYD	That's why I'm getting away on the oil rigs.
TONY	Did he actually kill the four . . . or was he just one of a group?
ALLEN	He was the hit man, he pulled the trigger . . . he was one of the top hit men.
TONY	I don't remember him being involved in a fight here.
BOYD	He was too small to fight.
ALLEN	He was afraid of everybody. Even in his last year he used to back down from second and third formers.
TONY	The people he killed . . . what ages were they, do you remember?
ALLEN	Young fellas.
BOYD	One of them was old . . . in his fifties.
TONY	Do you know anything about them?
ALLEN	Not much . . . two of them were claimed in death notices.
TONY	Ah yes, the justification. *(Long pause)* It's strange ... I'll spend the rest of my career looking for clues. Spot

the killers. I've thought about it before, once or twice. I've often wondered if "my" pupls were involved. My killers were always the lazy ... the dirty ... a profusion of pimples ... a dirty shit ... *(Pause)*
(The bell rings for the end of another period)

BOYD	It's still the same, isn't it?
TONY	Is it? Yes, I suppose it is.
BOYD	At least there'll be no bells on the oil rigs.
TONY	There are, you know.
BOYD	What . . . you're kidding me?
TONY	It's true, bells, hooters, the music of routine.
ALLEN	You'll never work on the oil rigs. He'll never go, sir. He hasn't even applied.
BOYD	D'you want to bet?
ALLEN	You've written away?
BOYD	I haven't written away yet, but I'm goin' to.
ALLEN	Aye, I hear you.
BOYD	I'll bet you a fiver.
ALLEN	A fiver! Where would you get a fiver!
BOYD	I'll be getting the address this week.
ALLEN	You're all talk. What's kept you up 'till now?
BOYD	I had to wait 'till I was eighteen.
ALLEN	You were eighteen months ago.
BOYD	Aye, you can't just write on your birthday, can you? That would look suspicious.
TONY	I hope you get away . . . if you need a reference . . .
BOYD	Oh, thanks very much . . . sir. See, oil boy, that's where the money is. Three hundred a week, no probs.
ALLEN	Who's goin' to pay you three-hundred a week? Wise it, son.
BOYD	It's true . . . isn't it, Mr Cairns?
TONY	I don't know exactly, but they say you can earn a lot of money.
BOYD	Three-hundred a week. Is that more than a teacher?
TONY	Yes, quite a bit more.
BOYD	There see, I don't need O Levels. The oil rigs, that's where it is . . . and there's no blinking oul War Poets either.
ALLEN	Ah, too dangerous them things. No wonder they pay so much. They're always blowing over. The boats ... that's the best.
BOYD	The boats! Sure them things is always sinking. I'd rather have an oul rig any day. Look at that oul Titanic ... hits a wee ice cube and the bloody thing sinks.
ALLEN	An ice cube! Did you ever hear the like of that

	ignorant get. It was an ice-berg . . . berg, son, berg.
BOYD	I don't care if it was a hamburg, it still sunk.
TONY	Right lads . . . what about a cup of tea or coffee?
BOYD	That'd be great . . . coffee for me.
TONY	Tom?
ALLEN	We'll have to go soon. *(Pause)* I'll take a cup of coffee please, sir.
TONY	Right . . . I'll have to nip along to the staffroom. It shouldn't take long. Milk and sugar?
ALLEN	Milk and two sugars please, sir.
BOYD	Milk and five sugars, sir.
TONY	Five spoonfuls of sugar?
BOYD	Seven if it's a big mug. I've a sweet tooth.
TONY	You are lucky to have any teeth at all at that rate. *(He goes)* *(Tony still out. Allen and Boyd snoop about. Are sitting when David enters)*
BOYD	Hey, not bad, eh? Cups of coffee and all. Probably chocolate biscuits.
ALLEN	Drinking out of a teacher's cup . . . we'll have to watch we don't get the pox.
BOYD	Hey, maybe he'll piss in it, try to poison us. Or maybe he'll rub the biscuits round his balls.
ALLEN	Ah for . . . will you shut up?
BOYD	You just watch and see if he eats any with us. You can't trust teachers.
ALLEN	He gets a bit excited about things, doesn't he?
BOYD	He gets excited? I thought you were cracking up the way you were screaming at him. You're lucky he didn't hit you a welt on the snout.
ALLEN	That's why I didn't want to say anything to him . . . I knew he'd flip. He was interested in all the details, wasn't he? 'Member when we used to do the War Poets, he used to love all the bits about blood and guts? *(He picks up a homework book)*
BOYD	Did you see his oul face when I said I'd be getting three hundred knicker a week?
ALLEN	Three hundred a week! My brother didn't get that much and he used to rob banks.
BOYD	Look at this . . . the cleaners must use this place as well. Hey . . . I wonder does he bring the cleaners in here for a wee bit, eh? Maybe he's a big box of frenchies stashed away . . . *(Looking around)*
ALLEN	He wouldn't need frenchies, the cleaners are oul dolls.
BOYD	What difference does that make?
ALLEN	The change . . . the change of life.

137

BOYD	*(Uncomprehending)* Oh . . . d'you mean he's good-living now?
ALLEN	Christ boy, you're looped. *(Pause)* Here, listen to this; "Wilfred Owens poem is about men and all and guns and shooting and bombs gassing and all he died of gas and choked in all green stuff and blood. I think it is a good poem because it tells you all about it and all and I think it's good so I do. Wilfred Owens was a soldier and he died in Armistice in the war so he did."
BOYD	That's good, who writ that?
ALLEN	Andrew Beattie.
BOYD	That's Ginger's wee brother. He must be doing O Level. He's probably going to be a teacher. *(The door is rapped and opened simultaneously. David Dunn enters)*
DAVID	Hello, what have we here? *(They scramble to their feet, afraid)* It's all right, no need to stand. Suit yourselves. Where's Mr Cairns?
ALLEN	He's gone to make some coffee, sir.
BOYD	Is he making you two coffee?
ALLEN	Yes, sir.
DAVID	Why is he doing that, are you blackmailing him?
ALLEN	No, air.
DAVID	Allen isn't it?
ALLEN	Yes, sir. Tom Allen, sir.
DAVID	And you're Boyd. Bill Boyd, known as Scout, because you used to keep dick when the boys were tossing themselves off in the bogs.
BOYD	I did not, sir . . . *(Dunn punches him lightly)* Ooohh . .
DAVID	Flabby stomach, Boyd. You're not in shape, eh?
BOYD	No, sir.
DAVID	I thought you were going to go off and become a world champion, wasn't that the plan?
BOYD	I give it up, sir.
DAVID	Typical, I supposed the first time your nose would bleed you'd be sickened. Gutless . . . that's the trouble with you lads.
BOYD	I'm going away you see, on the oil rigs, sir.
DAVID	The oil rigs, eh?
BOYD	I'm writing tomorrow, sir.
DAVID	Writing eh, who taught you to do that? You couldn't do it when you were here. It's nothing to grin about, boy.
BOYD	Three hundred quid a week sir. *(David punches him again)* Awe, that was sore, sir . . . sorry, sir.
DAVID	I should think so, Boyd. Three hundred quid a week!

138

	If I thought for one minute that you would earn more than me, I'd strangle you. Do you understand that, son?
BOYD	Yes, sir.
DAVID	Because you're not worth more than me, are you, son?
BOYD	No, sir.
DAVID	Allen, why were you looking at Mr Cairns' books, eh?
ALLEN	I was just having a wee look, sir. Just seeing if it's the same as we done, sir.
DAVID	"Did" son. The same as we "did".
ALLEN	The same as we did, sir.
DAVID	Of course it's the same, son. The same rubbish from the same sort of goons. It doesn't change you know. *(Pause)* So you're going on the oil rigs, Boyd? Thank God we've got the Arabs, that's all I can say. What about you, Allen, how have you decided to waste your life?
ALLEN	I'm not sure, I was thinking of the Merchant Navy, sir.
DAVID	Thinking, Allen, you were always thinking, never doing, just thinking, eh?
ALLEN	Yes, sir.
DAVID	So what are you doing whilst you think this little matter over?
ALLEN	I'm on the dole, sir.
DAVID	On the dole! Now that's a surprise. A lad of your ability, and after the fine education we gave you. Most young lads of your age are up to their eyes in muck and bullets now.
	(Cairns re-enters)
TONY	David.
DAVID	David? In front of the lads?
TONY	They're big boys now.
DAVID	Do you mean we can talk in front of them just like they were normal human beings?
TONY	We're short a cup. I'll nip back to the staffroom and fetch one.
DAVID	It's alright, Boyd will fetch me a cup, won't you Boyd? Run to the staffroom, knock on the door, and ask if you may borrow a clean cup for Mr Dunn, got that?
BOYD	Yes, sir.
DAVID	Boyd . . . if the said cup contains lipstick traces, or gunge, I'll shove it up your ass . . . clear?
BOYD	Yes, sir.
DAVID	Well, jump to it then. *(He goes)* Well, Onassis, I

	suppose you've crawled back up here to beg for a reference?
ALLEN	No sir, we just dropped in to see Mr Cairns.
DAVID	I see, and were you going to leave without calling in to see me?
ALLEN	I . . . we . . . I never thought, sir.
DAVID	You never thought, huh! When creatures like you start crawling back here to see me, I'll really begin to worry. *(Boyd returns with a cup, which he hands to David)* What is this, Boyd?
BOYD	It's ah . . . it's a cup, sir.
DAVID	A cup, brilliant Boyd. What's in it?
BOYD	It's clean, sir, no lipstick or that other stuff . . . *(Pause)* . . . Ah . . . there's nothing in it, sir, it's empty, sir.
DAVID	I'm a patient man, Boyd. I've waited over two years to get another opportunity to put my toe up your arse, but I'm not going to wait any longer. *(Grabbing Boyd by the ear)* Now if you're not back here in two minutes with that cup full, one sugar, no milk, some poor surgeon is going to have to don his rubber gloves and retrieve my shoe. *(He goes again)* Civility Tony, the only way with sensitive lads like these. *(Pause)* So you're on the dole, Allen?
ALLEN	Yes, sir.
DAVID	The best place for you.
TONY	Tom did have a job.
DAVID	Oh, Tom is it . . . excuse me. Where was the job?
ALLEN	In Mackies, sir, just labouring.
DAVID	What else, I didn't think you were the foreman. So why aren't you still there? *(Pause)*
TONY	He was paid off.
DAVID	Paid off! Sacked more like. Did they give you the boot?
ALLEN	Yes, sir. *(Boyd returns)*
DAVID	Good, now pass me the biscuits. So you were sacked, why? *(Pause)*
BOYD	He kicked the foreman in.
DAVID	What, was he a blind cripple with a hearing problem? Why did you hit your foreman? *(Pause)*
ALLEN	He insulted my sister, because she's married to a soldier.
DAVID	Was this foreman a Fenian?
ALLEN	Yes, sir.
DAVID	So you stuck one on him. A great blow struck for Protestant Ulster, eh? I'll bet he was a big Fenian too,

140

	an eight footer, post-famine, eh? Don't you admire these lads, Tony? They have wee Fenians for breakfast, don't you lads?
BOYD	I hate them, sir.
DAVID	Of course you do, Boyd and with you it's not just instinctive, it's the result of long intellectual rumination.
BOYD	Aye.
DAVID	You know what I used to tell my rugby lads? Imagine the person you're tackling is a dirty Fenian who has just raped your sister.
TONY	For goodness sake, David . . .
DAVID	Of course there was always the thick get who would tell you he didn't have a sister. *(Pause)* I hear Joe's retired to the country, Allen?
ALLEN	Yea, sir, he got fourteen years.
DAVID	It wasn't a Fenian he shot . . . a Protestant who works, almost as bad. *(Pause)* A brother inside, and a sister married to a Brit. Then we have Boyd here. I'll bet you're up to your dirty little neck in all kinds of nastiness, and you're one brother a peeler, and another a soldier. They're almost on the same side.
BOYD	I'm not in nothing, sir.
DAVID	Well, why don't you join up in something?
BOYD	Naw, sure I'm away for the oil rigs.
DAVID	How could I have forgotten? Tell me Allen, when can the world's waterways expect to be graced by your presence.
ALLEN	I'm not sure . . .
DAVID	You're still thinking?
TONY	It's not just a straightforward decision, David.
DAVID	I see, have you knocked some wee chewing-gum queen up the shoot? Can't drag yourself away from her pimpled brow and sweaty little knickers?
ALLEN	My da's not well, sir.
DAVID	Living with you I'm not surprised. What's supposed to be wrong with him?
ALLEN	He's dying, sir, with a bad heart. *(Pause)*
DAVID	Is that true?
TONY	(Angrily) Of course it's true, you don't think he'd make a thing like that up do you?
DAVID	Well, I didn't know that, lad. I knew he used to be ill, but I thought that was all cleared up. So there's just you and your mother? *(Pause. Tony gives him a look)* Right, I can't afford to hang about here any longer.

	There must be boys to be kicked in somewhere. I'll see you later, Tony. So long, lads.
ALLEN	Goodbye, sir.
BOYD	Be seeing you, sir. *(David goes. Pause)*
TONY	I'm sorry, Tom. He doesn't really mean any harm.
ALLEN	It's all right, sir. I had him for four years ... he wasn't bad.
BOYD	Wasn't bad? I'd love to bump into him up our way some night that's all. He hurt my belly.
ALLEN	Get him up our way! He'd kick you into orbit, son. He's the hardest man in this school ... isn't he, sir?
TONY	Well, I'd never thought about it, but yes I suppose he would be.
	(Long pause)
TONY	Roy's father, what sort of a man is he?
ALLEN	He's just ordinary.
BOYD	He used to be a big shot ...
ALLEN	But he left or something.
BOYD	They don't like him now anymore sir.
ALLEN	Aye, well look, sir, it's time we were heading ...
TONY	*(As they rise to go)* Listen you two ... Boyd, you get your letter off tonight ... and you, Tom ... *(Pause)*
ALLEN	I'll smother the oul fella.
TONY	Keep in touch. Come up again and let me know how it's going. If there's anything I can do to help ...
	(They shake hands and go)
	(Tony walking about room, David re-enters)
DAVID	Why does Monday seem to last forever?
TONY	That was quite something.
DAVID	The lads?
TONY	They told me all about Roy Alexander. We're completely out of touch.
DAVID	It's called a social conscience. I lost mine when our birthrate started to fall.
TONY	We've got to do something.
DAVID	Rifle ranges? Lessons in unarmed combat?
TONY	I'm beginning to wonder if what I'm doing in this classroom is of any value to anyone.
DAVID	The last teacher I heard talking like that committed suicide at the end of the week. *(Trying to break through Tony's gloom)* It's your pre-menopausal crusade. It could be worse. Fleming had his nervous breakdown. *(Pause)* It's called The Road to Damascus Syndrome. The last cheap thrill for the privileged classes. It's only a twenty-four hour thing.
TONY	I'm thinking of going round tomorrow night to have a

142

	word with Roy Alexander's father. Maybe I can help.
DAVID	Come on, Tony. That's not your area. If Roy Alexander is a murderer, you can bet his old man isn't captain of the local cricket club. What can you do for Roy Alexander, spring him?
TONY	His father was probably like Roy once. Maybe even had a teacher like me.
DAVID	For goodness sake, Tony . . . you are only a teacher . . . you do your best, you always have.
TONY	It has become painfully obvious that my best falls a long way short of what is required. If a patient given the wrong medication dies, the doctor is held responsible.
DAVID	So if someone throws a stone and breaks a window, you suggest we shoot the window cleaner? A Level English would not have changed Roy Alexander. You're being ridiculous. All right, so Allen and Boyd are failures. Their sisters are pregnant, brothers in jail, mothers living in sin and all the rest of it. Do we now blame all of that on their English teacher? You have taught them all your life and you have taught them well. You're the most conscientious, caring, professional teacher in this school . . . but you only serve the system. Damn it, if anybody should feel guilty it's me. I don't even work the system.
TONY	I watched you with those lads just now . . . they understood you . . . they understood you in a way they have never understood me.
DAVID	The wee shites hate the sight of me, always have.
TONY	No, they know you. They understand who you are and what you are.
DAVID	And what am I, Tony? I'm one of the few who seems to have beaten the system.
TONY	If you have . . . why not others?
DAVID	Because they are two different worlds and I'm not sure you can ever make the adjustment. It's chance not choice that makes the Roy Alexanders.
TONY	You're saying they can't be helped?
DAVID	Not by us. The Grand Canyon isn't as deep or as wide as the gap between what they need and what we give them.
TONY	So why do you do it?
DAVID	Me? I just do it for the few bob, it's the safest way.
TONY	So I suppose I should keep on teaching, just "for the few bob".

DAVID	Even if you did force a few minor changes through ... even that I doubt with that bollocks we have. Even if you do ... tiny little adjustments in one school ... so what?
TONY	I am not going to change the system, I know that. I am going to make my contribution relate to the pupils.
DAVID	*(Tiring of the argument)* No matter what you do, I'll still hate it.
TONY	Maybe you should look for another job?
DAVID	I should and in theory I do. The trouble is that not only do I hate this job, I also hate all the possible alternatives ... I can think of. Where else would you get the long holidays? *(Fade)*

INTERVAL

ACT TWO

SCENE 1

(Allen and Boyd are seen in the street)
(Alexander's house. Eric is searching under cushions etc. Ruby comes in from another part of the house)

RUBY	Did you find anything?
ERIC	Ten pee.
RUBY	How much do you have?
ERIC	Sixty-eight and ten . . . seventy-eight.
RUBY	Seventy-eight pee! It'll have to do. Get a loaf, milk and a tin of beans. We'll just have to go easy. Don't forget to keep some for the gas. I'll go and see Ellen tomorrow, she gets the family allowance.
ERIC	Are you sure he wouldn't let you have a few more things?
RUBY	It takes him all his time to serve me now even when I have the money.
ERIC	Bastard. I'd like to burn his bloody shop to the ground.
RUBY	It isn't his fault. He does what he's told like all the rest. *(Pause)*
	(He puts on his coat and they kiss)
ERIC	I'm away, I've a key so don't open that door to anybody.
RUBY	*(Hanging onto his hand)* Someday you'll walk out of here and they won't let you walk in again.
ERIC	Get that graveyard look out of your gub, and give my head peace.
	(He goes . . . out into the street. As he moves off Archie and Brickso approach him. Allen and Boyd are also seen)
ARCHIE	Hello Eric, how's the form?
ERIC	I'm all right.
ARCHIE	How's Roy?
ERIC	He's . . . he's all right.
ARCHIE	Must be lonely for him up there.
ERIC	He's all right, he's not on his own.
ARCHIE	For the rest of his life, it's a hard oul slog. *(Pause)* I ah . . . I hear you're leaving?

145

ERIC	Where'd you hear that?
ARCHIE	Ah, just somebody talking like, in the club. Somebody said you'd soon be away like. That was the talk.
ERIC	I've no plans to go anywhere.
ARCHIE	Aye well maybe it was just a rumour. It's a wild place for rumours, eh Brickso?
BRICKSO	That's what I heard too.
ERIC	Well, you heard wrong then. You'll not put me out.
ARCHIE	Us? We're not trying to put you out. Come on now, Eric, you don't think it's us do you?
ERIC	You're quare and bloody soft. I wouldn't trust bloody one of yous.
ARCHIE	It's hard to know who you can trust nowadays, isn't it? *(Pause)* The oul electric bills must be right and high with the lights on all day like?
ERIC	You'll not be asked to pay them so it needn't worry you.
ARCHIE	But we do worry about you, Eric. You used to be one of the lads, respected, well liked. It didn't have to change. I mean if it hadn't been strictly in the family ... if it wasn't for Roy ... your boarded up windies wouldn't save you. *(Pause)* How's Ruby? *(Allen and Boyd enter stage right)*
ERIC	She's all right.
ARCHIE	Must be an even bigger strain on her, all the aggravation and all.
BRICKSO	Nice woman Ruby. Tell her I was asking about her.
ERIC	Why all the concern for us now?
BRICKSO	Well, you'll probably not be with us for much longer, so ...
ERIC	Listen you, maybe you're deaf, or just stupid, but I said I wasn't going anywhere.
ARCHIE	Must have been a rumour. Only it was all over the club on Saturday night.
BRICKSO	Maybe it was another Eric and Ruby they were talking about?
ARCHIE	That's right, there must be thousands of Erics and Rubys around here. Could have been any of them.
ERIC	Now you bastards listen to me, I'm not even slightly concerned about you lot, let alone frightened. And if any of you ever lift a finger to Ruby ...
ARCHIE	If you're here Eric ... if you haven't left first. *(Pause)*
ERIC	Bastards. *(He pushes past them. They turn and gaze after him)*
ARCHIE	Now there goes one unhappy man.
BRICKSO	There goes one frightened man.

ARCHIE	I used to like Eric, he was a good commander.
BRICKSO	Too soft, always saw that in him. He used to be near sick when he went to a rompering.
ARCHIE	Why did he do it? I mean that's what I don't understand, his own son.
BRICKSO	If he did that to his own son, what'd he do to the rest of us? He should've been hit months ago. I mean he could be going to the cops right now to blow the works.
ARCHIE	Who's going to hit him, that's the trouble?
BRICKSO	I wouldn't fancy bein' the one who hit Roy's oul lad.
BOYD	Don't look at me . . . I couldn't shoot anybody.
ALLEN	Sure Roy's away for good . . . they'll never let him out.
ARCHIE	He's got friends but. *(Pause)*
ALLEN	You should have heard oul Eric this morning when we rapped the door.
BRICKSO	Suppose you disturbed him screwing Ruby.
ARCHIE	Christ boy, I'd love to screw that. 'Member in the bar . . . the big tits, the arse. I wish now I'd chanced my arm.
BRICKSO	Huh, she wouldn't have let you near her if you'd had diamonds round it.
ARCHIE	She only fancied Eric 'cause he was the commander.
ALLEN	He's not the commander now, so why's she staying?
ARCHIE	If they bump Eric off there's goin' to be a quare randy woman on the loose, and I'll have those tits for ear muffs.
BOYD	And if she's on the change you'll not even need a frenchie. *(They look at him)* *(Fade)*

SCENE 2

(Allen and Boyd on the street. As Tony approaches they run off into the darkness. As Tony appears Archie steps out into his path)

ARCHIE	You lost or something, mate?
TONY	I was looking for Roy Alexander's house.
ARCHIE	Roy doesn't live here anymore, he's on holiday.
TONY	His father still lives here I believe.
ARCHIE	*(Over Tony's shoulder)* You got a line on him, Brickso?
BRICKSO	*(Off)* Right between the shoulder blades, no probs.

147

ARCHIE	Why don't you just go back where you come from?
BOYD	*(Approaching)* He's all right, Archie. I know him. He's Mr Cairns.
ARCHIE	Who's Mr Cairns?
BOYD	Mr Cairns is our oul English teacher. He's all right. It's all right Brickso, it's our oul teacher. *(Brickso emerges from the shadows)* Brickso's my uncle.
TONY	Really, and he was just about to shoot me?
BRICKSO	Ah . . . *(Points a water pistol at Tony and squirts it in his face)* . . . *(They laugh, Tony wipes his face)* . . . What are you doin' round here?
ARCHIE	He's looking for Alexander's place.
BRICKSO	Oh . . . it's not a very popular place.
TONY	Why is that? I would have thought Roy might be a bit of a hero around here.
ARCHIE	Roy's all right. Roy's one of the lads. It's his oul fella, nobody likes him. He done something . . . ask no questions . . .
TONY	I see, well I wanted to see him to talk about Roy. Would you show me where he lives? *(Pause)*
BOYD	Mr Cairns'll be all right, lads . . . they'll not say nothing about him . . . school teacher and all that.
TONY	Do you mean that people are not allowed to visit Mr Alexander?
ARCHIE	It's not that they're not allowed, they're advised against it. We like to know who's coming and going like. You're just lucky Scout was with us the night. If he wasn't here it could have been rough on you.
TONY	I only want to talk to the man.
BOYD	*(Slightly puffed up)* It'll be all right, lads. *(Pause. Points)* That's it over there, Mr Cairns.
TONY	*(Pause)* Thanks . . . goodnight.
ARCHIE	We'll say goodnight when you're leaving, mate.
BOYD	See you, Mr Cairns.
	(Tony goes. Allen joins the others from the shadows. They look after Tony. As lights come up on house, they go. Ruby sitting lost in thought when Tony knocks. She shouts from the hallway.)
RUBY	Yes, what do you want?
TONY	I was wondering if I could speak to Mr Alexander.
RUBY	Who are you?
TONY	I'm a friend of Roy's. That is, I was. I used to be his teacher.
RUBY	Roy's not here.
TONY	I know that, I was hoping to talk to Mr Alexander about him

148

| | *(Pause) (Opens door)* |
| RUBY | You'd better come in for a minute. *(They enter. She closes the door)* Eric ... Eric ... there's somebody here to see you. *(Pause. Louder)* Eric ... Eric ... *(She goes out of the room. Off)* Eric ... Eric ...
(Off. He hits her. She cries out in pain and staggers back into the room, holding her mouth. He follows her in. He is extremely nervous, carrying a gun) |
ERIC	What have I told you about just opening that door to anybody? *(To Tony)*
TONY	I'm Tony Cairns.
ERIC	What do you want and what are you?
TONY	I'm a school teacher . . . I taught Roy.
ERIC	Oh aye, never much time for school teachers myself. Clever asses the lot of you. Think you know it all.
RUBY	Eric . . . Mr Cairns is a gentleman.
ERIC	You keep your mouth closed . . . unless you want another crack on it. What would you know about gentlemen? We're going to have bloody barmaids telling us who the gentlemen are now.
TONY	I'm sorry, it's my . . . I didn't mean to alarm you.
ERIC	Who's alarmed? Me? I don't scare easy, mister. Could have got you killed. I might have plugged you thinking you were here to get me. Stupid bitch . . . I've told her. *(To Ruby)* I've told you never to open that door until you're sure. Here, come and see, mister ... *(Takes Tony to inspect the door)* Look, tins, bean cans, peas, biscuit tins, all sorts of things hammered flat and nailed to that door. That's to protect that silly bitch, 'case somebody fires through the door when she goes to open it.
TONY	Yes, I saw the nails on the outside.
ERIC	Never mind the nails on the outside, it's the protection inside I'm worried about.
TONY	Mr. Alexander, I wanted to talk to you about Roy.
ERIC	Roy's left school a long time ago.
TONY	I know, I've been . . . out of touch. I only learnt yesterday about Roy's trouble.
ERIC	Trouble . . . what are you talking about?
RUBY	Have a seat Mr Cairns. Would you like some tea, Mr Cairns? Will I make some tea, Eric?
ERIC	You said trouble.
RUBY	I'll make some tea. *(She goes)*
TONY	I was wondering if I could help in any way?
ERIC	Mister, you'd better start explaining what you mean by trouble? *(Pause)*

149

TONY	I only heard yesterday about Roy's imprisonment, Mr Alexander.
ERIC	Never mind "Mr Alexander" . . . do you have any childer?
TONY	I have two. My son's an historian. My daughter's studying to be a doctor.
ERIC	What's a historian do?
TONY	Well . . . he studies and writes about history.
ERIC	My son's a hero, mister. My son makes history. *(Pause)* My Roy was fearless, mister, heart like a lion. I'll tell you something about my Roy. If he'd been told to go down to the bottom of North Street and shoot a man with blue eyes, he's an IRA man — he'd have done it, in broad daylight. And if there'd been ten men with blue eyes, he'd have shot them all . . . just to make sure. He was fearless.
TONY	Roy was always a very quiet boy at school. I was quite surprised.
ERIC	You know nothing about him. When he was sentenced he never flinched, he stuck his fist in the air and shouted "no surrender". *(Pause)* I was a proud man.
TONY	He killed people . . . other men's sons.
ERIC	*(After a long pause)* He executed enemies. We're at war. He could have been shot himself. He'd have died a hero.
TONY	Does his mother visit him?
ERIC	Oh, you bloody school teachers know it all . . . snooping, asking kids about their personal business. *(pause)* He wouldn't let his ma near him. She writ him letters. Told him to give himself to the Lord, look to Jesus. Lot of good he's done us. He told me about them . . . we had a good laugh. *(Pause)*
TONY	What does he do in jail?
ERIC	Everybody round here was afraid of him. There were no tins on the door when Roy was here. There'll be some changes when he gets out again.
TONY	I thought I might write to him. He might consider doing his A Levels. I could help him . . . with books and things.
ERIC	Books and things! What does my son want with books? He's a hero, a man of action. Stick your books where the English stuck our constitution.
RUBY	*(Coming in with the tea and serving it out)* Help yourself to milk and sugar. No biscuits, I'm afraid.

150

	We're waiting for Eric's boroo to come through. That wee scone's for you.
TONY	It's all right, Mrs . . . ?
ERIC	Mrs nothing . . . she's Ruby. I don't need any missus. Could have had a dozen women if I'd wanted. They listened to me when Roy was here. I was something then.
TONY	Neither of you work then?
ERIC	Don't you come in here to ask us questions. School teacher! Always asking questions. Prying. That's all school teachers are good for. Prying and preaching . . . perfect people and the rest of us are scum.
TONY	We try to help the pupils.
ERIC	Oh aye, what would you lot know about help? D'you think my Roy needs help? By the time he gets out the right people'll be running this country. He'll be all right . . . a pension, well looked after.
RUBY	Is your tea all right, Mr Cairns?
TONY	It's fine, thank you.
RUBY	Are you sure you won't have that wee scone?
TONY	No, I'm fine, thank you. It's a very nice cup of tea.
ERIC	*(Rising)* Piss.
TONY	Mine's all right.
ERIC	*(Pointedly to him)* I said I'm going for a piss. *(Goes)*
RUBY	He's not too well . . . it's his nerves. He's not usually like this. We give him a fright, that's all . . . he thought you were someone coming for him.
TONY	Why are they after him? If Roy is such a big hero, surely . . .
RUBY	Heroes! There've been heroes shot dead in that club, heroes kicked to death in streets like this. In this town you can go to bed one night a hero and wake up the next morning as public enemy number one. *(Long pause)*
TONY	Why do you stay here in these awful conditions? What is there to stick it out for?
RUBY	We'll be moving soon . . . moving, or be moved . . . *(Eric returns. Pause).*
TONY	*(Rising)* I think I'll go. If I left my address Mr Alexander, would you give it to Roy?
ERIC	Oh aye, you'd have him on his knees too, praying for forgiveness. Keep you address, mister.
TONY	He could write to me if he thought I could help.
ERIC	Leave my son alone. Roy's doing all right. *(Pause)*
TONY	Goodbye Ruby, thank you for the tea. Mr Alexander? *(Offers his hand)*

151

ERIC	*(Refusing the hand)* Go on, go on. *(To Ruby)* You go and lock that door after him.
RUBY	Good night Mr Cairns.
TONY	Good night, and thank you again. *(Tony goes. Pause)*
RUBY	I'm sorry, Eric.
ERIC	It's all right, love. I'm sorry I hit you. *(pause)* I thought it was somebody to get me. When I heard you coming in I thought you were trying to act natural, that he had a gun on you. I even thought you were setting me up for it. *(Pause)* My stomach just churned up. I sweated, thought I was going to be sick. Thought I was going to drity myself. I don't even think I could have used that gun ... *(Pause)* I wanted to cry. I didn't want to die and I thought it was all such a waste. *(Long pause)* We'll go now, love.
ERIC	Go ... you mean leave ... get out ... honestly?
ERIC	Don't say a word to anybody ... not even your Ellen. When the giro comes on Thursday, we'll just leave. It'll get us to Liverpool. We can worry about the rest when we get that far.
RUBY	I love you, Eric. I can work ... in a bar again. We can live ...
ERIC	Sssshhh. *(Silence)*
RUBY	Why didn't you tell him, Eric? Why didn't you tell that Mr Cairns?
ERIC	Tell him ... tell him that my son was a mad dog. Tell him that I betrayed my son ... informed on him? *(Pause)* He'd have really loved that. He would have told me how fine and responsible I was. I could have cried into his tweed shoulder pad. If you encourage that lot, God knows what poor murderer's da they'd start pestering next. I bring Roy books, that's all I can do for him, and he would take even that away from me. If only he'd given my son some sort of education ... it was a personal thing anyway. The only personal thing ever between me and my son. He's his mother's now, on his knees, singing hymns, making me say prayers with him.
RUBY	He'll never come back here, love, even if they did let him out, you know that.
ERIC	Why didn't he hate me for it? I could understand that. Why doesn't he hate me.
RUBY	Don't cry, Eric ... please. *(Pause)*
ERIC	*(Rising and controlling himself with great effort)* We could have gone weeks ... months ago. We stuck it

152

out for nothing. The bastards ... the lousey, rotton
bastards.
(Fade)

SCENE 3

*(Staffroom. Winifred and Frank are already at their
lunch)*

FRANK We'd better be going out together on Friday afternoon
and start gathering what we need for this kitchen of
yours.

WINIFRED Oh, it'll be great to get it done . . . you really are a
love. Of course, I'll make you your meals while you're
at it.

*(Tony enters from the alcove with his tea and sits. They
stop talking, exchanging a little smile. Tony opens his
sandwiches as David enters)*

TONY I thought you were going to try the canteen today?

DAVID Mince and turnips. The bowels haven't been built that
can stand up to that. *(Throwing his sandwiches on a
table)* Chicken paste, if you're going to be sick on shit,
be sick on familiar shit. What have you today, Frank?

FRANK Uh? Egg and onion.

DAVID Jasus, don't be farting in room seven. I've to use it
after you. *(Pause)* Well, Tony, how was your trip to
Disneyland last night to see Alexander's da?

TONY It wasn't very pleasant.

DAVID You were warned. So Da Alexander wasn't quite a
gentleman?

WINIFRED Home visits, Tony, I admire your commitment. I feel
that when I get through here I've given my pound of
flesh.

TONY Well, I suppose I shouldn't have arrived uninvited.
They live like animals, and they seem to think the
same way.

DAVID You don't think they need help?

TONY Try it, it's like trying to feed slices of roast beef to a
crocodile, by hand.

DAVID For a while on Monday I thought you had gained a
few insights into social deprivation or whatever.

TONY So did I, but that was a sympathetic response.

DAVID So it's all hands on deck and stand-by to repel
boarders. The good ship apathy sails again.

153

TONY	You have this habit, David, of confusing frivilous banter with serious debate. I am not saying we don't have to act, far from it. My approach was wrong. My failure was with Roy Alexander.
WINIFRED	Roy Alexander, isn't he the one who murdered fourteen people?
TONY	He murdered four people.
WINIFRED	Four! I thought it was fourteen. I'm sure it was fourteen.
DAVID	You're mixing him up with Alexander the Great, Winnie.
FRANK	Murdered four people. Was he a pupil here?
TONY	Yes, one of the better ones too. He was one of your star history pupils. A very small, dark haired boy, quiet, quite clean and tidy.
FRANK	Oh, I don't remember, they all look alike to me.
DAVID	Through the bottom of a glass darkly.
TONY	He murdered four Roman Catholics.
WINIFRED	Maybe he had good reason to. Perhaps they were IRA men.
TONY	Perhaps Jesus was a member of the PLO.
DAVID	She's right, Tony, one of them was the transport officer for the IRA.
TONY	How do you know that?
DAVID	He had a bicycle pump on him.
TONY	Is there any point trying to have a serious discussion in here. I want to see some changes. I think we have all got to sit down and take a long hard look at ourselves and what we are doing. Too many of our pupils are leaving here inadequately prepared for any meaningful role in society.
WINIFRED	You can only work with the material to hand.
TONY	No, Winifred, it's more complex than that. Whenever we do think about our failure rate it is always thrown back on the pupils. It's time we really put things in perspective. We really need to do something for these pupils.
FRANK	With all due respect, Tony, I've done all I can throughout my career.
WINIFRED	Likewise, I've given my life to teaching. I know they're from poor backgrounds, that many of them are underprivileged. God, you only have to have a nose in your head to realise that, but you've known that for years, we all have.
TONY	I haven't really, that is my whole point. Yes I should have. The fault lies entirely with me. I should have

154

	known. The pupils were our victims. Any blame rests very clearly on us.
FRANK	I refuse to accept that. Do you know how many years I've given to teaching? All this new fangled nonsense about teachers failing ...
TONY	I have already spoken to Mr. Montgomery, and he seems to agree with me.
FRANK	You have spoken to Mr Montgomery?
TONY	Indeed. He said he would drop in at lunchtime and we could all have a quiet informal discussion.
DAVID	Jasus, if the chicken paste doesn't make me sick, that get will.
FRANK	Tony, I've served my sentence, almost. Whatever my debts to society, I've repaid them with interest. I have three years left to go, I'm too old for crusades.
TONY	You have taken me up wrong, Frank. I'm not criticising you as Frank Mercer, I'm criticising you as a teacher. That is where our collective responsibility lies.
WINIFRED	The responsibility lies with their parents for having them.
DAVID	Jasus, Winnie, apart from your birth, that's the nearest you've ever come to cracking a joke.
TONY	Come on, David, leave the banter aside. There are serious issues that we really do need to start sorting out our thoughts on.
DAVID	My dear chap, after your remarks about Mr Alexander I assumed your educational revolution had been stillborn.
TONY	Mr Alexander is beyond our help but we have got to make some attempt to stop the rot. I'm talking about each of us feeling that at least, in so far as we can as individuals, we are addressing the problems and doing our best.
FRANK	Supposing we feel that already? *(Pause)*
TONY	Then it is up to those of us who know better to highlight the true facts.
FRANK	Really, Tony, this is outrageous. You are attacking my integrity. Dress it up whatever way you like, that is what you are doing. What price loyalty?
TONY	Come on, Frank, you know better than that. Loyalty cannot be confused with wilful blindness.
FRANK	Wilful?
TONY	Yes. I feel that we have a lot to offer in terms of ideas and practice. Where do our true loyalties lie?
FRANK	You are saying to me that I can admit my faults and

155

	failings. I can bare my soul, confess, as it were. If I fail to do that then you are going to expose me.
WINIFRED	That's rather high-handed action, Tony.
TONY	Maybe that underpins one of our greatest failings. We stick to this code of professionalism, of narrow loyalty. Maybe it would be no bad thing for us to hold ourselves up to general scrutiny. Each classroom tends to be an independent republic and no one interferes in the internal affairs of another "country". It is wrong. We're making ourselves too comfortable.
FRANK	Too comfortable? Surely if the Headmaster is satisfied, it ill becomes you to criticise. I mean, well damn it, you have no authority.
TONY	The Headmaster has a role to play, but we are all professionals.
WINIFRED	Are you suggesting we inform on each other?
TONY	I'm not suggesting we spy or inform on each other. I am suggesting a system, a structure within this school that will make that unnecessary. I'm saying that we sit down and thrash things out, we take collective decisions and we share overall responsibility.
	(Herbert knocks and enters. He's carrying a cup of tea)
HERBERT	Have you been talking to them, Tony?
TONY	Only in general terms, about the need to start seriously questioning what we are doing here.
HERBERT	*(Ignoring David)* If I can just throw in one or two of Tony's ideas for a first response. Tony wants to incorporate the Remedial Department within the English Department and make all, or at least most teachers responsible for some remedial work.
WINIFRED	That is my department, Mr Montgomery.
TONY	I'm keen to break down this silly mystique about most remedial teaching being outside the experience and competence of all but a few, specially trained experts. With all due respect, Winifred is Head of the Remedial Department, yet she has had no special training.
WINIFRED	Mr Cairns . . . really . . . I bring a lifetime's experience and I've attended numerous courses over the years.
TONY	You've attended a few, infrequent seminars at teacher centres. If we all adjudged ourselves to be remedial teachers to some extent, with effort and exchanging ideas, pooling our experience, I'm sure we could make considerable inroads on our problems.
WINIFRED	Well, I for one will oppose it. I will fight you tooth and nail on this one. *(Pause. She points at David)* There's a member of your own department who

156

	refuses to set homeworks. Whose pupils are handed over to me, because he can't cope with them. Is he going to be one of your remedial "experts"?
DAVID	I'd make a better job of it than you, you old bollocks. At least I wouldn't have anti-teaching headaches six times a day.
WINIFRED	I will not agree, Mr Montgomery, and I will expect ... indeed, I will demand your support.
HERBERT	At the moment I'm only floating Mr Cairns' ideas for initial comment. *(Pause. Pleased at the unfavourable response)* Another suggestion is that we abolish subject division in the first two or three years and teach a humanities course that would include English, History and Geography. For history the third year should be given over to the teaching of Irish history, to the exclusion of all else.
FRANK	Irish history? What absolute nonsense, it doesn't deserve comment.
TONY	Mr Montgomery, I must protest. You are presenting my ideas in the worst possible light.
HERBERT	I'm being concise, but accurate am I not?
TONY	What I suggest initially is team teaching of English, History and Geography for the first two years. Then, after a suitable running-in period of about two years, the departments could blend into a Humanities Department ...
FRANK	With you as head of it!
TONY	No, with a separate head, a new post. Whoever was in charge of it would have full charge of all pupils in those first two crucial years.
FRANK	If you want power, why don't you go and apply for a Vice Principalship like anyone else?
TONY	I don't want power ...
FRANK	You don't want to compete for it, you want to create your own power-base in here. You want to abolish Winifred's post, abolish my post and set yourself up as academic dictator.
TONY	You are getting things out of perspective. If I can be given time to explain ...
FRANK	It's quite clear to me. It all fits with your talk before Mr Montgomery came in. Outrageous, sir, outrageous.
TONY	Look, these are my ideas, constructive proposals for discussion. If you disagree, fine, but counter my proposals with some of your own, don't just dismiss them.
FRANK	It's a pity we couldn't just dismiss you for having

them. The third year given over to Irish History. I
suppose you'd like us to decorate the classroom with
framed photographs of De Valera ... and ... and ...
and ... Patrick Pearse. Is that the next of it?

TONY   I suggested Irish History, not republican history. There
is a difference, you should know that.

FRANK   I know it, yes, I know it, but do the republicans know
it? No wonder our boys shoot them. To them Irish
history is a catalogue of their rights and our wrongs.
You can get yourself a teaching post in Dublin if
that's the sort of nonsense you want to teach. *(At
David)* Maybe he could fix you up on one of his
weekend whoring trips. Irish history, huh.

WINIFRED Terrible, terrible, he's treating us like criminals to be
punished for a lifetime's dedication and loyal service.

TONY   Let's all just calm down a minute. In third year, our
pupils select subjects for themselves. If they drop
history, and many of them do, then they leave this
school without ever having learnt anything about the
history of their own country. That is immoral. I want
a full year of twentieth century Irish History. It is
surely important for them to know about how this
state came into existence, and why it exists. I think we
have a duty to enlighten them on such vital matters.

DAVID   I agree one hundred per cent.

FRANK   You would, you could send them out to start a riot for
homework.

HERBERT   Actually you wouldn't be involved, Mr Dunn. Mr
Cairns envisages the setting up of a sin-bin. You
would have charge of that and overall responsibility
for discipline. You might do a little teaching in an area
loosely defined as moral philosophy.

DAVID   Moral philosophy?

HERBERT   Yes, that would replace Religious Education in the
upper school.

TONY   You see, David, my concern is the idea that the only
morality is Christian morality. In our circumstances, I
feel that is dangerous. Do you really want people like
Roy Alexander to feel that not being a Christian
absolves him from acting in a moral way.

DAVID   Thanks Tony, but no bloody thanks. If I want to be a
screw I'll apply to the Maze, and if I want to be a lay
preacher I'll join the Free Presbyterians.

TONY   *(To Herbert)* You have quite deliberately presented my
ideas in the worst possible light. Now they will become

158

	the subject of ill-informed gossip and never be seriously assessed or discussed.
HERBERT	Not at all, I've tried to be as objective and fair as possible. After all, the most important reaction would ultimately be my own. Frankly, these reactions reflect my own.
TONY	I feel very strongly that we must act.
HERBERT	You can act, in your capacity as Head of English. Anything outside of that is not your responsibility.
TONY	It is not enough for one person to tamper. We all need to address ourselves to the problems.
	(The bell sounds for the end of lunchtime)
DAVID	*(At the door)* You got your kick on the balls . . . *(Looking pointedly at Herbert's feet)* . . . but he forgot the slippers. *(Goes)*
HERBERT	Are you two free now?
WINIFRED	No, no, we were just going.
FRANK	Irish history, huh.
	(Winifred and Frank exit)
TONY	You have done me a grave disservice today, Herbert.
HERBERT	What you have failed to appreciate is my overall responsibility for what happens in this school. Criticism for the way we do things here is criticism of me. You have been severely critical and I strongly resent that.
TONY	I've had a rude awakening, Herbert.
HERBERT	You're being over emotional about all of this, Tony. I'll return your folder . . . drop in at three-thirty.
TONY	What?
HERBERT	You've seen the reaction for yourself. We're teachers, Tony. You cannot treat social problems through a school curriculum. We might wish education was valued for its own sake, but it's not. People want papers, certificates, diplomas, degrees. Our job is to equip as many people as possible to acquire those documents.
TONY	*(Ignoring his hand)* I'm going to have to think things over carefully. I'm not prepared to carry on as if nothing had happened. You sat in that office and gave me the impression that you fully endorsed everything I was saying. Then you come in here and actually attempt to humiliate me.
HERBERT	You're exaggerating, Tony.
TONY	No, I am not.
HERBERT	Yes you are. Tony. I listened to you, as I listen to everyone. All members of staff get a fair hearing from

159

	me. I didn't endorse what you were saying. I think, given our pupils and given this area we do a very fine job. I'm very proud of my staff and my school, I've fought and struggled to get where I am today and I've fought and struggled to put this school where it is. I'm not one to discourage improvements provided they're not at variance with the curriculum.
TONY	All right, all right, you've made your point. *(Pause)* Now I'll make mine. This school is a shambles. We are turning out sixteen year olds who can barely read or write. I have often defended you, but your critics are right. You function as a PR man. Everything is for show. As for your struggle ... you got where you are today because you played the system. A system that would revolt any man of principle. You joined the right organisations. You went to the right church and even sent your wife and children to others ... just to be sure. You even started teaching in Sunday School.
HERBERT	How dare you ... now just ...
TONY	I'm stripping off the dark glasses of professionalism ... in future I will speak out. Whatever I see wrong I will shout about. About Winifred and her convenience headaches. About Frank and his laced flask. About bullying incidents when pupils are seriously injured, yet you keep out the ambulance and police to protect the school's "good name". If the parents knew the half of what goes on here they'd run you out of town.
HERBERT	Now just a minute, Tony ...
TONY	*(Out front)* Look ... down there ... filthy hovels full of Allens and Boyds ... dole fodder ... sent out of here trade-marked "failure" ... This school mass-produces semi-illiterate morons. Multiply this by the thousands of others and you have a compulsory education system that patents failure. That is what we are a party to, and nobody even wants to discuss improvements. *(Pause)*
HERBERT	*(Coldly)* Impressive rhetoric, Mr Cairns. The system has served you well enough for years though ... *(Tony makes a gesture of despair)* ... and so have I. Don't forget you're Head of English today thanks to me.
TONY	Then that is obviously the place to start. You can find yourself another Head of English, as of now. *(Long pause. They stare at each other. Tony picks up a pile of books and walks out)* *(Fade)*

SCENE 4

(The living room. Ruby is packing. Eric enters with a suitcase and places it with two others)

ERIC	I never knew we'd so many clothes.
RUBY	If there's anyone about when we go out, Eric, just ignore them.
ERIC	Don't go on about that.
RUBY	I just want to get away quietly. I don't want any more fuss. I've had enough.
ERIC	I'll have to lift a tile in the yard and bury that gun. *(The door is banged loudly. They stiffen)*
ALLEN	*(Off)* Come on, Alexander, open the door. We want to talk to you. *(Pause)* We'll give you two minutes and then we're coming in. *(Eric is shaking)*
ERIC	Let them in.
RUBY	For God's sake, Eric, don't be a fool. Let's just go away, Eric. Please, Eric ... please ...
ERIC	Will you open the bloody door, they're not going to let us walk away.
BOYD	Come on, Alexander ... we know you're in there.
ERIC	*(Shaking, almost in tears)* Open the door, woman ... please. Look, love, they're no keener to die than I am. Open the door and when they're all in you run out and slam the door behind you.
RUBY	No ... not without you, Eric ...
ERIC	*(As they bang the door again)* Open it before they knock the bloody thing down. *(Pause. She goes)* *(He moves to the far side of the room, concealing the gun. She opens the door and the two come in. She closes the door behind them and locks it. Pause)*
ALLEN	They'd like a word with you, Eric.
ERIC	Tell them they've got what they wanted, Tom. We're going ... for good.
ALLEN	That was yesterday's answer, Eric ... things have changed.
ERIC	Just let us walk out that door an' you can tell them they'll never hear tell of us again.
ALLEN	Naw, until the next swoop.
ERIC	Swoop ... what swoop?
ALLEN	Five of our lads were lifted that day.
BOYD	Somebody squealed.
ERIC	I know nothing about it ... it wasn't me.
ALLEN	You can tell them that.
ERIC	Come on, Tom.

BOYD	Cut out the oul chat.
ERIC	If they get me inside that Club I'll never come out alive, you know that.
BOYD	If you're innocent ...
ERIC	I'm not going.
ALLEN	These aren't walking sticks, Eric ... you either come now or we'll drag you down.
BOYD	You put Roy inside ...
ERIC	He was my son, I'd the right to do it.
ALLEN	How many sons have you got? *(He takes a step towards Eric. To Boyd)* You take that oul bag ...
ERIC	*(Shaking violently and producing the gun)* The next one of you who moves'll find his brains next door.
BOYD	It's not a real one.
ERIC	Isn't it? You step forward and prove it. Drop those sticks on the sofa and turn around, face the door, both of you. Move. *(Eric is so nervous that the gun is as likely to go off by accident. They realise this and are nervous themselves)*
ALLEN	Mr Alexander, it's not us, honest to God. We didn't want to ... they made us.
BOYD	That's the God's truth ... I was Roy's friend ... we sat beside each other in school. Don't shoot ... please don't shoot ...
ERIC	Shut up gerning the pair of you. I wish my Roy'd been as gutless as you two.
ALLEN	We didn't want to come ... we're not really in it ... you know that.
ERIC	I've had nightmares about you lot ... but it was always Archie I saw. He'd crash through the door and come charging up the stairs ... I let him halfway up before I shot. It was as plain as now ... a big hole where his left eye used to be. *(Raising the gun)* Stop bloody snivelling.
ALLEN	Don't shoot us, Eric ... sure you know my da ...
BOYD	Stop him, missus ... Ruby ... please, missus ... for Jasus sake.
RUBY	Don't shoot them, Eric. *(Long pause)*
ERIC	Start taking your clothes off, now ... everything.
BOYD	In front of her?
ERIC	Would you rather be shot in front of her. Now, come on, move. *(Pause. They start to undress)* The longer I stand here tensed up, the more likely my finger is to just snap on this trigger. Come on. Get me your sleeping tablets, Ruby.
RUBY	What?

ERIC   You heard me, get me your sleeping tablets. You're
        not going to need them anymore. And get me a glass
        of water *(Ruby exit to kitchen for water and tablets,
        returns and leaves them on the suitcases)* Keep your
        underpants on. Now take their clothes out and put
        them in the bin.
BOYD   Ah, come on, Eric. Them's my good trousers, the oul
        doll'll kill me.
ERIC   Somebody will, that's for sure . . . and if you don't
        shut up it'll be me. Take the firelighters love, make
        sure everything burns . . . shoes and all
ALLEN   We'll get you for this, Eric . . . *(Ruby goes)* . . . you'll
        not get away with this. *(Pause)* Those bloody clothes
        cost money.
ERIC   If you knew how much I'd love to send a bullet
        crashing through your stupid skull . . . you'd be too
        grateful to still be standing there to worry about
        anything else. *(Eric is calmer now)* Archie's not going
        to be too happy with you two, is he? Right . . . get four
        of them tablets each . . . wash them down with the
        water. *(They do so)*
BOYD   If I die, my ma'll think I took an overdose.
ERIC   She'll wonder why you stripped to do it . . .
        everybody'll think you're two queers. *(He laughs . . .
        They don't)* I don't think four of them'll do yous much
        harm. *(Ruby returns)* We'll wait until these two
        bastards are sleeping comfortably . . . then we'll go.
        (Fade)

SCENE 5

*(As lights fade, Tony enters. Moves downstage into light
at the front. If possible the light should in some way
connect him to the street. He has a book in his hand. He
looks weary . . . regards his class. Pause. He pulls
himself up)*

TONY   *(Sharply)* Pay attention . . . Beattie, turn around and
        sit up straight. *(Pause. Reads)*
            "These are the damned circles Dante trod,
            Terrible in hopelessness,
            But even skulls have their humour,
            An eyeless and sardonic mockery:
            And we,

163

Sitting with streaming eyes in the acrid smoke,
That murks our foul, damp billet,
Chant bitterly, with raucous voices
As a choir of frogs
In hideous irony, our patriotic songs."
(Pause. The school bell rings . . . the noise of school getting out. Tony closes the book, holds it limply at his side, bows his head as the lights fade)

RUBY   I'm catching that boat, Eric. If you do go back, then you'll have to kill those two boys. Either that or them or their mates will kill you. It's a vicious circle and getting on that boat is the only way to break it.
(Long pause, Eric slowly picks up the cases and they go)
(Fade lights as they exit, bring up lights in house to see the two boys sleeping)
(Fade light for final curtain)

SCENE 6

(This should be set on an anonymous area of the stage. Eric and Ruby are hurrying along with their suitcases . . . Eric with two, Ruby with one. They stop to rest)

RUBY   There it is, we've made it. *(Eric sets down his cases)* What's wrong?
ERIC   I'll never see him again, Ruby.
RUBY   You'll maybe be able to get back now and again.
ERIC   No, I'll never be able to come back, never. What was it all for?
RUBY   Eric . . . come on, for Jesus sake, come on. You came very close to murdering those two tonight . . . doing what Roy did . . . becoming what he is.
ERIC   I can't go . . .